BLESS THE LORD!

Companion volumes by the same author

For the ordinary season of the year . . .
(Epiphany to Lent and Pentecost to Advent):

PRAISE HIM!
A Prayerbook for Today's Christian

For the seasons of Advent, Christmas, Lent and Easter:

BLESS THE LORD!
A Prayerbook for Advent, Christmas,
Lent and Eastertide

t/

BLESS THE LORD!

A PRAYERBOOK FOR ADVENT, CHRISTMAS, LENT AND EASTERTIDE

Edited by

William G. Storey, D.M.S.
t/
Director, Graduate Program in Liturgical Studies
University of Notre Dame

AVE MARIA PRESS

Notre Dame, Indiana 46556

ACKNOWLEDGMENTS:

The Jerusalem Bible, © 1966 by Darton, Longmans & Todd, and Doubleday and Company, Inc., for Old Testament readings and canticles. Used by permission of publisher.

The American Bible Society for New Testament readings from *Good News for Modern Man,* © 1966; and for psalms from *The Psalms for Modern Man,* © 1970.

International Consultation on English Texts, © 1970: the Lord's Prayer, the Apostles' Creed, Doxology, Te Deum, Canticle of Zachary and Canticle of Mary.

International Committee on English in the Liturgy, © 1973: Act of Contrition, Alma Redemptoris, 38 Advent-Christmas collects, one collect from the Masses of the Departed, the collects of St. Joseph and St. John the Baptist.

Community of St. Mary the Virgin, Wantage, England: "For Perfect Charity."

Archbishop Joseph Raya and Baron Jose de Vinck, *Byzantine Daily Worship* (Allendale, N.J.: Alleluia Press, 1969): "Christmas Eve," Troparion of Preparation.

Rev. Norman W. Goodacre, *Prayers for Today* (London: Mowbrays, 1972): "An Ancient Salutation to the Blessed Virgin Mary."

Canon Charles M. Guilbert, Custodian, Standard Book of Common Prayer of the Episcopal Church, *Prayers, Thanksgivings and Litanies* (Prayerbook Studies, 25): "For Families." All rights reserved. Used by permission.

A. Hamman, O.F.M., Early Christian Prayers (Chicago: H. Regnery, 1961): "Prayer to the Mother of God" of Balai of Aleppo.

Jean Vanier, *Eruptions to Hope* (Paramus, N.J.: Paulist-Newman, 1971): "As My Heart Opens Up."

Rev. Laurence Mancuso, *Book of Hours* (New Canaan, CT: Holy Protection Monastery, 1965): "Great Canon" of St. John of Damascus.

Nicholas of Cusa, *The Vision of God* (New York: Frederick Ungar): "To Christ Our Sole Teacher."

Rev. Dr. John Webster Grant, *The Hymn Book of the Anglican Church of Canada* (Toronto, 1971): Translation of the "Veni Creator Spiritus."

Nihil Obstat: Charles J. Ueber
      Censor Deputatus

Imprimatur: Most Rev. Leo A. Pursley, D.D.
      Bishop of Fort Wayne-South Bend

ISBN 0-87793-076-7 (paper)
      0-87793-077-5 (cloth)

Art by Kathryn Kelly

Printed in the United States of America

CONTENTS

CONTENTS

PREFACE

One of the main thrusts of the modern biblical and
liturgical revival is to remind Christians that their
prayer book *par excellence* is the Book of Psalms. If
Christians really want to learn how to pray, how to put
on the mind of Christ, how to correspond prayerfully
and resolutely to all the ups and downs of Christian
existence, they have only to take up the Psalter, "the
perfect form of prayer for the layman" (Thomas
Merton). But to do so fruitfully one needs to grasp the
fact that the Psalms are "full of the Incarnate Word"
(Merton). On a superficial, historical level, the
Psalter is a very old Jewish collection of cultic hymns
and personal poetry. On a more profound level, it is
a Christian prayer book, thoroughly assimilated to the
gospel after two thousand years of liturgical and
private use. To Christian believers initiated into the
Church's way of praying, the Psalms speak everywhere
of Christ—living, dying, rising, coming again. They
find fulfillment in the hearts of those who believe that
the Paschal Mystery is the clue to human existence.

PREFACE

This present *seasonal* prayer book is a sequel and companion to *Praise Him!* (Ave Maria Press, 1973). It is designed to highlight and interpret the Psalms in the context of the four strong seasons of the liturgical year: Advent, Christmas, Lent, Easter.

It does this by linking psalms and a variety of biblical canticles with New Testament antiphons, psalm prayers, brief readings from both Testaments, and forms of intercessory prayer.

This book is designed primarily, but not exclusively, for personal use and is meant to be employed with freedom and spontaneity. Its resources are not so much controls as guides and suggestions from the rich and many-layered tradition of Catholic piety. Small groups and families may find this book useful to spark common prayer in the morning and evening, before or after meals. It is hoped that it will be particularly helpful to the old, the sick and the bedridden.

William G. Storey, D.M.S., Director
Graduate Program in Liturgical Studies
University of Notre Dame

SUGGESTIONS FOR USE

1. Before beginning to *say* morning or evening prayer, make a serious, personal effort to stand in the presence of the Blessed Trinity, who created and redeemed you and who dwells by grace in the depths of your soul. God is always present to you; be present to him by loving attentiveness and by a keen desire to go on, day after day, "seeking his face." Many Christians find a quiet, intense use of the Jesus Prayer a helpful prelude to all attempts at vocal prayer. (See Appendix, p. 239.)

2. Call upon the indwelling Spirit, the only true teacher of prayer, and say the opening versicles.

3. Recite the morning or evening psalm or canticle with meditative care and devotion. The New Testament antiphons that often accompany these texts should help draw these Old Testament passages into the fuller context of the gospel.

After reciting the psalm or canticle, pause for a few moments to meditate on it, in whole or in part, or simply to recollect yourself gently but insistently in the abiding presence of God.

At the end of the silent prayer, say the collect prayer that sums up, interprets and applies the psalm or canticle.

9

4. Read the short lesson from scripture, mull it over a bit and listen to what God has to say personally to you through it. A two-year "Table of Scripture Readings" will be found in an appendix for those who would like longer and daily readings throughout the four seasons. (See Appendix, page 241.)

5. Short versicles lead into the Gospel Canticle of Zachary or Mary with their appropriate seasonal antiphons.

6. Each evening has a seasonal form of intercession. Spontaneous prayers may, of course, be added to or substituted for the litanies provided.

7. Each act of worship closes with the two most basic of all Christian prayers, the Apostles' Creed and the Lord's Prayer. They should be said with a maximum of attention and concentration, as befits their special dignity. Even if compelled to omit all else, a faithful Christian should begin and end each day of his or her life with these noblest acts of commitment and prayer.

GROUP PRAYER

When these forms of morning and evening prayer are used in common, it is helpful to have both a *leader* and a *reader*.

The designated *leader* should

—call the group to prayer with the opening versicles
—lead the psalm or canticle (see below)
—call for silent prayer and pray the psalm prayer
—initiate the versicles after the reading
—lead the gospel canticle
—recite the petitions of the litany (evening)
—pray the closing prayer
—lead the Creed and the Lord's Prayer

The designated *reader* should read the short lesson printed out in the text or the longer lesson indicated in the "Table of Scripture Readings" (Appendix, page 241).

Group Recitation of the Psalms and Canticles

Psalm 19[a] (Advent: Sunday Morning, page 16) may be used as an example of four possible ways of reciting the psalms:

1. Responsorially:
The *leader* recites the antiphon:
"You are the bright and the morning star, O Christ our Lord."

All repeat it immediately, again after each stanza, and finally after the concluding doxology.

The text of the psalm itself is said by the *leader* alone.

2. Antiphonally: stanza by stanza

The *leader* recites the antiphon and then alternates the psalm stanza by stanza (strophe by strophe) with the participants.

All repeat the antiphon after the psalm.

3. Antiphonally: verse by verse

The *leader* recites the antiphon and then alternates the psalm verse by verse with the participants.

Leader: How clearly the sky reveals God's glory!
How plainly it shows what he has done!

All: Each day announces it to the following day;
each night repeats it to the next.

Occasionally the verses are composed of a triple parallelism instead of the usual double, but they are recited in the same way:

Leader: God set up a tent in the sky for the sun;
it comes out like a bridegroom striding
from his house,
like an athlete, eager to run a race.

All: It starts at one end of the sky
and goes around to the other.
Nothing can hide from its heat.

All repeat the antiphon after the psalm.

4. Unison Recitation:

All recite the entire psalm with its antiphon in unison.

Variety in the use of these four styles of psalmody should challenge the ingenuity of any group praying the psalms regularly.

There is only one physician,
   both carnal and spiritual, born and unborn,
   God become man, true life in death:
   sprung both from Mary and from God,
   first subject to suffering and then incapable of it
   —Jesus Christ our Lord.

                              St. Ignatius of Antioch

**All seasons are fruitful for Christians,
for all are full of Jesus Christ.**

Bossuet

ADVENT

ADVENT—Sunday Morning

Blessed is he who comes in the name of the Lord.
Hosanna in the highest!
O Lord, open my lips.
And my mouth shall declare your praise.

Psalm 19ª: Christ Is the Sun of Righteousness

Ant. You are the bright and the morning star, O Christ
our Lord.

How clearly the sky reveals God's glory!
How plainly it shows what he has done!
Each day announces it to the following day;
each night repeats it to the next.
No speech or words are used,
no sound is heard;
yet their voice goes out to all the world,
their message reaches the ends of the earth.

God set up a tent in the sky for the sun;
it comes out like a bridegroom striding from his
house,
like an athlete, eager to run a race.
It starts at one end of the sky
and goes around to the other.
Nothing can hide from its heat.

Glory to the Father and to the Son and to the Holy
Spirit;
as in the beginning, so now, and for ever. Amen.

Ant. You are the bright and the morning star, O Christ
our Lord.

16

Psalm Prayer

Let us pray (pause for silent prayer)
To enlighten the world, Father,
you sent us your Word
as the sun of truth and justice
shining upon mankind.
Illumine our minds that we may discern your glory
in the many works of your hands.
We ask this through Christ our Lord.
   Amen.

Reading   **Rm 13:11-14**

You know what hour it is: the time has come for you to wake up from your sleep. For the moment when we will be saved is closer now than it was when we first believed. The night is nearly over, day is almost here. Let us stop doing the things that belong to the dark. Let us take up the weapons for fighting in the light. Let us conduct ourselves properly, as people who live in the light of day; no orgies or drunkenness, no immorality or indecency, no fighting or jealousy. But take up the weapons of the Lord Jesus Christ, and stop giving attention to your sinful nature, to satisfy its desires.

Response

The sun of righteousness will rise.
   With healing in his wings.

Canticle of Zachary   **Lk 1:67-79**

Ant. The Lord will visit his people in peace.

Blessed be the Lord, the God of Israel;
   he has come to his people and set them free.
He has raised up for us a mighty Savior,
   born of the house of his servant David.

17

Through his holy prophets he promised of old
    that he would save us from our enemies,
    from the hands of all who hate us.
He promised to show mercy to our fathers
    and to remember his holy covenant.

This was the oath he swore to our father Abraham,
    to set us free from our enemies' hand,
free to worship him without fear,
    holy and righteous in his sight
    all the days of our life.

You, my child, shall be called the prophet of the Most
      High,
    for you will go before the Lord to prepare his way,
to give his people knowledge of salvation
    by forgiveness of their sins.

In the tender compassion of our God
    the dawn from on high shall break upon us,
to shine on those who dwell in darkness and the
      shadow of death,
    and to guide our feet on the road to peace.

Glory to the Father and to the Son and to the Holy
      Spirit;
    as in the beginning, so now, and for ever. Amen.

Ant. The Lord will visit his people in peace.

Morning Prayer

All-powerful God,
increase our strength of will for doing good
that Christ may find an eager welcome at his coming
and call us to his side in the kingdom of heaven,
where he lives and reigns with you and the Holy Spirit,
one God, for ever and ever.
 Amen.

Apostles' Creed   **Lord's Prayer**

The sign of the cross shall appear in the heavens
  when our Lord shall come to judge the world,
  and the servants of the cross,
  who conformed themselves here in this life
  to Christ crucified on the cross,
  shall go to Christ their judge
  with great faith and trust in him.
                              The Imitation of Christ

ADVENT—Sunday Evening

The Word had life in himself.
And this life brought light to men.

Psalm 85: A Prayer for the Nation's Welfare

Ant. His name is Emmanuel, the prince of peace.

Lord, you have been kind to your land;
 you made Israel prosperous again.
You have forgiven your people's sins
 and pardoned all their wrongs.
You stopped being angry with them
 and put away your furious rage.

Bring us back, God our Savior,
 and stop being displeased with us!
Will you be angry with us forever?
 Will your anger never cease?

Please renew our strength,
 and we, your people, will praise you.
Show us your constant love, Lord,
 and give us your saving help.

I am listening to what the Lord God is saying;
 he promises peace to us, his own people,
 if we do not go back to our foolish ways.
Surely he is ready to save those who honor him,
 and his saving presence will remain in our land.

Love and faithfulness will come together;
 righteousness and peace will meet.
Man's loyalty will reach up from the earth,
 and God's righteousness will look down from heaven.

The Lord will make us prosperous,
 and our land will produce rich harvests.
Righteousness will go before the Lord,
 and prepare the path for him.

Glory to the Father and to the Son and to the Holy
    Spirit;
  as in the beginning, so now, and for ever. Amen.

Ant. His name is Emmanuel, the prince of peace.

Psalm Prayer

Let us pray (pause for silent prayer)
God of love and fidelity,
you loved the world enough
to give your only Son as Savior
and from a virgin brought him forth to the world.
May we receive him as both Lord and brother
and celebrate him as our gracious redeemer.
He lives and reigns for ever and ever.
  Amen.

Reading   **Phil 4:4-7**

May you always be joyful in your life in the Lord. I
say it again: rejoice! Show a gentle attitude toward all.
The Lord is coming soon. Don't worry about anything,
but in all your prayers ask God for what you need,
always asking him with a thankful heart. And God's
peace, which is far beyond human understanding, will
keep your hearts and minds safe, in Christ Jesus.

Response

The angel Gabriel brought the message to Mary.
  And she conceived by the power of the Holy Spirit.

Canticle of Mary   **Lk 1:46-55**

Ant. O Wisdom, O holy Word of God,
         the whole created universe lies throbbing
            in your strong and gentle hand:
         Come, show us how to live.

21

My soul proclaims the greatness of the Lord,
    my spirit rejoices in God my Savior;
for he has looked with favor on his lowly servant,
    and from this day all generations will call me blessed.

The Almighty has done great things for me:
    holy is his name.
He has mercy on those who fear him
    in every generation.

He has shown the strength of his arm,
    he has scattered the proud in their conceit.
He has cast down the mighty from their thrones,
    and has lifted up the lowly.
He has filled the hungry with good things,
    and sent the rich away empty-handed.

He has come to the help of his servant Israel,
    for he remembered his promise of mercy,
The promise he made to our fathers,
    to Abraham and his children for ever.

Glory to the Father and to the Son and to the Holy
        Spirit;
    as in the beginning, so now, and for ever. Amen.

Ant. O Wisdom, O holy Word of God,
        the whole created universe lies throbbing
            in your strong and gentle hand:
        Come, show us how to live.

Let Us Pray

Let us call joyfully on Christ, the happiness of all who
        wait for him:
    Come, Lord, do not delay.

Joyfully, we await your coming.
   Come, Lord Jesus.
You existed before all the ages.
   Come, save us in this present age.
You created the world and all who dwell in it.
   Come, receive back the work of your hands.
You did not shrink from our death.
   Come, snatch us from death's dominion.
You came that we might have more abundant life.
   Come, give us life eternal.
You desired to gather all men into your kingdom.
   Come, show us your face.

(spontaneous prayer)

Evening Prayer

Father,
creator and redeemer of mankind,
you decreed and your Word became flesh,
born of the Virgin Mary.
May we come to share the divinity of Christ,
who humbled himself to share our human nature,
for he lives and reigns with you and the Holy Spirit,
one God, for ever and ever.
   Amen.

Apostles' Creed   **Lord's Prayer**

Prayer is the key of morning and the bolt of evening.
                                                    Gandhi

FOR PERFECT CHARITY

My God, I desire to love you perfectly,
With all my heart, which you made for yourself,
With all my mind, which you alone can satisfy,
With all my soul, which longs to soar to you,
With all my strength, my feeble strength
which shrinks from so great a task
and yet can choose nothing else
but spend itself in loving you.
Claim my heart; free my mind;
Uplift my soul; reinforce my strength;
That where I fail, you may succeed in me
and make me love you perfectly,
through Jesus Christ, my Lord.

Community of St. Mary the Virgin, Wantage

ADVENT—Monday Morning

Blessed is he who comes in the name of the Lord.
  Hosanna in the highest!
O Lord, open my lips.
  And my mouth shall declare your praise.

Canticle of Isaiah (2:2-5): Jesus Christ Is the Prince of Peace

Ant. All the nations will come and adore you.

In the days to come
  the mountain of the Temple of the Lord
shall tower above the mountains
  and be lifted higher than the hills.

All the nations will stream to it,
  peoples without number will come to it and say:
"Come, let us go up to the mountain of the Lord
  to the temple of the God of Jacob
that he may teach us his ways
  so that we may walk in his paths;
since the law will go out from Zion,
  and the oracles of the Lord from Jerusalem."

He will wield authority over the nations
  and adjudicate between many peoples;
they will hammer their swords into ploughshares,
  their spears into sickles.
Nation will not lift sword against nation,
  there will be no more training for war.

Glory to the Father and to the Son and to the Holy
    Spirit;
  as in the beginning, so now, and for ever. Amen.

OFFICE OF WORSHIP
ARCHDIOCESE OF ST. LOUIS

Ant. All the nations will come and adore you.

Collect Prayer

Let us pray (pause for silent prayer)
God of love,
you have established our Lord Jesus Christ
as the sovereign peacemaker and reconciler.
Free all the world to rejoice in his peace,
to glory in his justice and to live in his love.
We ask this through the same Christ our Lord.
  Amen.

Reading   Mi 2:12-13

Yes, I am going to gather all Jacob together, I will
gather the remnant of Israel, bring them together like
sheep in the fold; like a flock in its pasture they will
fear no man. He who walks at their head will lead
the way in front of them; he will walk at their head,
they will pass through the gate and go out by it; their
king will go on in front of them, Yahweh at their head.

Response

They will see the Son of Man coming in the clouds.
  With great power and glory, alleluia.

Canticle of Zachary   See page 255

Ant. See the King comes, master of the earth;
      he will shatter the yoke of our slavery.

26

Morning Prayer

Lord our God,
help us to prepare for the coming of Christ your Son.
May he find us waiting, eager in joyful prayer.
We ask this through Christ our Lord.
   Amen.

Apostles' Creed   **Lord's Prayer**

There are two kinds of people one can call reasonable:
   those who serve God with all their heart
      because they know him
   and those who seek him with all their heart
      because they do not know him.
                            Blaise Pascal

ADVENT—Monday Evening

The Word had life in himself.
  And this life brought light to men.

Psalm 48: Zion, the City of God

Ant. Here God dwells among men. (Rv 21:3)

The Lord is great, and must be highly praised
  in the city of our God, on his sacred mountain.
Zion, the mountain of God, is high and beautiful;
  the city of the great king brings joy to all the world!
God has shown that there is safety with him
  inside the fortresses of the city.

The kings gathered together
  and came to attack Mount Zion.
When they saw it they were surprised;
  they were afraid and ran away.
There they were seized with fear and anguish,
  like a woman about to bear a child.

We have heard about what God has done,
  and now we have seen it
in the city of our God, the Lord Almighty;
  he will keep the city safe forever.

Inside your temple, God,
  we think of your constant love.
You are praised by people everywhere,
  and your fame extends over all the earth.

You rule with justice;
  let the people of Zion be glad!
You give right judgments;
  let there be joy in the cities of Judah!

Walk all around Mount Zion and count its towers,
    take notice of its walls, and examine its fortresses,
so that you may tell the next generation
    that this God is our God, forever and ever;
    he will lead us for all time to come.

Glory to the Father and to the Son and to the Holy
        Spirit;
    as in the beginning, so now, and for ever. Amen.

Ant. Here God dwells among men.

Psalm Prayer

Let us pray (pause for silent prayer)
Lord God,
you raised your Son from the dead
and made him a temple not formed by human hands
and the heavenly protector of the new Jerusalem.
Make this holy city here below,
composed of living stones,
shine with spiritual luster
and witness to virtue among the nations.
We ask this through Christ our Lord.
    Amen.

Reading   **Phil 3:18-21**

I have told you this many times before, and now I repeat it, with tears: there are many whose lives make
them enemies of Christ's death on the cross. They are
going to end up in hell, for their god is their bodily
desires, they are proud of what they should be ashamed
of, and they think only of things that belong to this

world. We, however, are citizens of heaven, and we
eagerly wait for our Savior to come from heaven, the
Lord Jesus Christ. He will change our weak mortal
bodies and make them like his own glorious body,
using that power by which he is able to bring all things
under his rule.

Response

Hail, Mary, full of grace, the Lord is with you.
   Blessed are you among women, alleluia.

Canticle of Mary   **See page 256**

Ant. O sacred Lord of ancient Israel,
         who showed yourself to Moses
            in the burning bush,
         and gave him the holy law on Sinai:
         Come, stretch out your mighty hand and set us
            free.

Let Us Pray

In confidence let us pray to Christ our Redeemer who
         came to save mankind:
   Come, Lord Jesus.
In the mystery of our flesh you revealed your divinity.
   Give us new life by your coming.
You took our weakness upon yourself.
   Show mercy toward us.
By your humble first coming you redeemed the world.
   Free us from guilt when you come again.
You are blessed and alive and the king of all.
   Bring us into our eternal inheritance.
As you sit at the right hand of the Father.
   **Gladden the souls of the dead with the light of your
      countenance.**

(spontaneous prayer)

Evening Prayer

All-powerful God,
renew us by the coming in the flesh of our Savior
and free us from every trace of sin.
Grant this through Christ our Lord.
   Amen.

Apostles' Creed   **Lord's Prayer**

The knot of Eve's disobedience was loosed
   by the obedience of Mary.
   for what the virgin Eve had bound fast
      through unbelief,
   this did the Virgin Mary set free
      through faith.

St. Irenaeus of Lyons

TO THE BLESSED VIRGIN MARY

Under your protection we take refuge,
  O holy Mother of God;
  accept our petitions in our hour of need
  and deliver us from all dangers,
  O ever-glorious and blessed Virgin.

Hail, Mary, full of grace, the Lord is with you.
  Blessed are you among women.

O God, through the motherhood of the
    Blessed Virgin Mary,
  you bestowed the gift of salvation on
    mankind;
  grant that we may feel the intercession of
    her
  through whom we were privileged to
    receive the Author of life,
  Jesus Christ, your Son, our Lord,
  who lives and reigns with you and the Holy
    Spirit,
  one God, for ever and ever.
    Amen.

ADVENT—Tuesday Morning

Blessed is he who comes in the name of the Lord.
Hosanna in the highest!
O Lord, open my lips.
And my mouth shall declare your praise.

Canticle of Isaiah (11:1-9): Jesus, the Messianic King of Peace

Ant. His princely title reads: God-is-with-us.

A shoot springs from the stock of Jesse,
a scion thrusts from his roots:
on him the Spirit of the Lord rests,
a spirit of wisdom and insight,
a spirit of counsel and power,
a spirit of knowledge and of the fear of the Lord.
The fear of the Lord is his breath.

He does not judge by appearances,
he gives no verdict on hearsay,
but judges the wretched with integrity,
and with equity gives a verdict for the poor of the land.
His word is a rod that strikes the ruthless,
his sentences bring death to the wicked.

The wolf lives with the lamb,
the panther lies down with the kid,
calf and lion cub feed together
with a little boy to lead them.
They do no hurt, no harm,
on all my holy mountain,
for the country is filled with the knowledge of the Lord
as the waters swell the sea.

Glory to the Father and to the Son and to the Holy Spirit;
as in the beginning, so now, and for ever. Amen.

Ant. His princely title reads: God-is-with-us.

Collect Prayer

Let us pray (pause for silent prayer)
God our Father,
maker and lover of peace,
to know you is to live,
and to serve you is to reign.
Protect us from the violence and anarchy of our sins
and make us genuine disciples of the Prince of Peace.
We ask this through the same Christ our Lord.
  Amen.

Reading   **Is 7:10-14**

Once again Yahweh spoke to Ahaz and said, "Ask Yahweh your God for a sign for yourself coming either from the depths of Sheol or from the heights above." "No," Ahaz answered, "I will not put Yahweh to the test." Then he said: "Listen now, House of David: are you not satisfied with trying the patience of men without trying the patience of my God, too? The Lord himself, therefore, will give you a sign. It is this: the maiden is with child and will soon give birth to a son whom she will call Immanuel."

Response

Your light will come, O Jerusalem;
  The Lord will dawn on you in radiant beauty.

Canticle of Zachary   **See page 255**

Ant. He will be called Immanuel: God-is-with-us.

Morning Prayer

Father,
you show the world the splendor of your glory
in the coming of Christ, born of the Virgin.
Give us true faith and love
to celebrate the mystery of God made man.
We ask this through the same Christ our Lord.
  Amen.

Apostles' Creed   **Lord's Prayer**

The whole mystery of the spiritual life is
    that Jesus is forever being born in us.
  The whole meaning of being a Christian is
    to become bit by bit transformed into Jesus Christ.
                                          Jean Danielou

ADVENT—Tuesday Evening

The Word had life in himself.
And this life brought light to men.

Psalm 50:1-15: Genuine Worship

Ant. True worshipers will worship the Father in spirit
and in truth. (Jn 4:23)

The Almighty God, the Lord, speaks;
he calls to the whole earth, from east to west.
God shines from Zion,
the city perfect in its beauty.

Our God is coming, but not in silence;
a raging fire is in front of him,
a furious storm around him.
He calls heaven and earth as witnesses
to see him judge his people.
He says, "Gather my faithful people to me,
those who made a covenant with me by offering a
sacrifice."
The heavens proclaim that God is righteous,
that he himself is judge!

"Listen, my people, and I will speak;
I will testify against you, Israel.
I am God, your God.
I do not reprimand you because of your sacrifices
and the burnt offerings you always bring me.
And yet, I do not need bulls from your farms,
or goats from your flocks,
because the animals of the woods are mine
and the cattle on thousands of hills.
All the wild birds are mine
and all living things in the fields.

"If I were hungry I would not tell you,
because the world and everything in it is mine.

Do I eat the flesh of bulls,
    or drink the blood of goats?

"Let the giving of thanks be your sacrifice to God,
    and give the Almighty all the offerings that you
       promised.
Call to me when trouble comes;
    I will save you, and you will praise me."

Glory to the Father and to the Son and to the Holy
    Spirit;
    as in the beginning, so now, and for ever. Amen.

Ant. True worshipers will worship the Father in spirit
    and in truth.

Psalm Prayer

Let us pray (pause for silent prayer)
Your servant Jesus Christ became obedient unto death,
Almighty Lord and God,
and so pleased you more than all the holocausts of old.
Accept the sacrifice of praise we offer you through him
and grant that it may perfect the offering of our spirit.
Through the same Christ our Lord.
    Amen.

Reading   **1 Thes 5:1-8**
The Day of the Lord will come like a thief comes at
night. When people say, "Everything is quiet and
safe," then suddenly destruction will hit them! They
will not escape—it will be like the pains that come
upon a woman who is about to give birth. But you,
brothers, are not in the darkness, and the Day should
not take you by surprise like a thief. All of you are
people who belong to the light, who belong to the day.
We are not of the night or of the darkness. So then, we

should not be sleeping, like the others; we should be awake and sober. It is at night when people sleep; it is at night when people get drunk. But we belong to the day, and we should be sober. We must wear faith and love as a breastplate, and our hope of salvation as a helmet.

Response

Let the clouds rain down the Just One.
   And the earth bring forth a savior.

Canticle of Mary   **See page 256**

Ant. O flower of Jesse's stem,
           every eye is held by you;
           every prince and foreign power
           bows in silent worship to your beauty:
           Come, let nothing keep you from our rescue.

Let Us Pray

Let us pray to Christ our Redeemer, the way, the truth and the life:
   Come and stay with us, Lord.
Jesus, Son of the Most High, whose coming was revealed to the Virgin Mary by the angel Gabriel,
   Come and rule your chosen people.
Holy One of God, in whom John rejoiced while still in his mother's womb,
   Come and bring joy to all the earth.
Jesus, whose precious name was revealed to Joseph by an angel,
   Come and save your people from their sins.
Light of the world, awaited by old Simeon and the prophetess Anna,
   Come and comfort your people.
(spontaneous prayer)

38

Evening Prayer

Lord,
fill our hearts with your love.
And as you revealed to us by an angel
the coming of your Son as man,
so lead us through his suffering and death
to the glory of his resurrection,
for he lives and reigns with you and the Holy Spirit,
one God, for ever and ever.
   Amen.

Apostles' Creed   Lord's Prayer

FOR SOCIAL JUSTICE

Almighty and eternal God,
may your grace enkindle in all men
a love for the many unfortunate people
   whom poverty and misery reduce to a
      condition of life
   unworthy of human beings.
Arouse in the hearts of those who call you
   Father
a hunger and thirst for social justice
   and for fraternal charity in deeds and in
      truth.
Grant, O Lord, peace in our days,
peace to souls, peace to families, peace to our
   country,
and peace among nations.
   Amen.

Pope Pius XII

ADVENT—Wednesday Morning

Blessed is he who comes in the name of the Lord.
Hosanna in the highest!
O Lord, open my lips.
And my mouth shall declare your praise.

Canticle of Isaiah (35:1-7, 10): God Comes to Save Us

Ant. Hosanna to the Son of David! Hosanna in the
highest! (Mt 21:9)

Let the wilderness and the dry-lands exult,
let the wasteland rejoice and bloom,
let it bring forth flowers like the jonquil,
let it rejoice and sing for joy.

The glory of Lebanon is bestowed on it,
the splendor of Carmel and Sharon;
they shall see the glory of the Lord,
the splendor of our God.

Strengthen all weary hands,
steady all trembling knees
and say to all faint hearts,
"Courage! Do not be afraid.
Look, your God is coming,
vengeance is coming,
the retribution of God;
he is coming to save you."

Then the eyes of the blind shall be opened,
the ears of the deaf unsealed,
then the lame shall leap like a deer
and the tongues of the dumb sing for joy;
for water gushes in the desert,
streams in the wasteland,
the scorched earth becomes a lake,
the parched land springs of water.

They will come to Zion shouting for joy,
    everlasting joy on their faces;
joy and gladness will go with them
    and sorrow and lament be ended.

Glory to the Father and to the Son and to the Holy
    Spirit;
    as in the beginning, so now, and for ever. Amen.

Ant. Hosanna to the Son of David! Hosanna in the
    highest!

Collect Prayer

Let us pray (pause for silent prayer)
Father,
creator and redeemer of mankind,
you decreed, and your Word became man,
born of the Virgin Mary.
May we come to share the divinity of Christ,
who humbled himself to share our human nature,
for he lives and reigns with you and the Holy Spirit,
one God, for ever and ever.
    Amen.

Reading   **Is 9:5-7**

For there is a child born for us, a son given to us and
dominion is laid on his shoulders; and this is the name
they give him: Wonder Counselor, Mighty God,
Eternal Father, Prince of Peace. Wide is his dominion
in a peace that has no end, for the throne of David and
for his royal power, which he establishes and makes
secure in justice and integrity. From this time onward
and for ever, the jealous love of Yahweh Sabaoth will
do this.

Response

Show us your constant love, Lord.
  And give us your saving help.

Canticle of Zachary   **See page 255**

Ant. You shall bear a son and call him Jesus,
      Son of the Most High God will be his title.

Morning Prayer

Heavenly Father,
you appointed your only-begotten Son
to be the savior of the human race
and commanded that his name be called Jesus;
may we who respect and venerate his holy name on
    earth
come to see him face to face in heaven.
We ask this through the same Christ Jesus our Lord.
  Amen.

Apostles' Creed   **Lord's Prayer**

**The most pressing duty of Christians is
    to live the liturgical life
and increase and cherish its supernatural spirit.**
                                        Pope Pius XII

ADVENT—Wednesday Evening

The Word had life in himself.
And this life brought light to men.

Psalm 67: The Messianic Harvest

Ant. May the peoples praise you, God;
may all peoples praise you.

God, be merciful to us and bless us;
look on us with kindness,
that the whole world may know your will;
that all nations may know your salvation.

May the peoples praise you, God;
may all peoples praise you!

May the nations be glad and sing for joy,
because you judge the peoples with justice
and guide all the nations.

May the peoples praise you, God;
may all peoples praise you!

The land has produced its harvest;
God, our God, has blessed us.
God has blessed us;
may all people everywhere honor him.

Glory to the Father and to the Son and to the Holy
Spirit;
as in the beginning, so now, and for ever. Amen.

Ant. May the peoples praise you, God;
may all peoples praise you!

Psalm Prayer

Let us pray (pause for silent prayer)
Look on us with kindness, Lord,
and give us your boundless mercy and lasting blessing.
Help us to profess your name with reverence and awe
and so bring forth a harvest for everlasting life.
We ask this through Christ our Lord.
   Amen.

Reading   Jas 5:7-9

Be patient, then, my brothers, until the Lord comes.
See how the farmer is patient as he waits for his land to
produce precious crops. He waits patiently for the
autumn and spring rains. And you also must be
patient! Keep your hopes high, for the day of the
Lord's coming is near. Do not complain against one
another, brothers, so that God will not judge you. The
Judge is near, ready to come in!

Response

I am coming soon, says the Lord.
   Amen! Come, Lord Jesus!

Canticle of Mary   See page 256

Ant. O Key of David,
          O royal Power of Israel
          controlling at your will the gate of heaven:
          Come, break down the prison walls of death
          and lead your captive nations into freedom.

Let Us Pray

Let us pray to the Lord who is coming to save us:
   Come and save us.
Lord Jesus, anointed One of God,
   Come and save us.
You came forth from the Father into our world,
   Come and save us.
You were conceived by the power of the Holy Spirit,
   Come and save us,
You took flesh in the womb of the Virgin Mary,
   Come and save us.
Savior of the living and of the dead,
   Come and save us.

(spontaneous prayer)

Evening Prayer

Come, Lord Jesus,
do not delay:
give new courage to your people who trust in your
   love
and by your coming raise us to the joy of your king-
   dom,
where you live and reign with the Father and the Holy
   Spirit,
one God, for ever and ever.
   Amen.

Apostles' Creed   **Lord's Prayer**

Remaining with the Father the Word is truth and life:
By clothing himself in our flesh he becomes the way.
                              St. Augustine of Hippo

THE JOYFUL MYSTERIES OF THE ROSARY

1. Hail, Mary . . . and blessed is the fruit of your womb, Jesus, whom you conceived of the Holy Spirit.
2. Hail, Mary . . . and blessed is the fruit of your womb, Jesus, at whose coming John the Baptist jumped for joy.
3. Hail, Mary . . . and blessed is the fruit of your womb, Jesus, who was born in Bethlehem of Judea.
4. Hail, Mary . . . and blessed is the fruit of your womb, Jesus, whom you presented in the temple.
5. Hail, Mary . . . and blessed is the fruit of your womb, Jesus, whom you found sitting in his Father's house.

Pour forth, O Lord,
  your grace into our hearts,
  that we to whom the incarnation of Christ
      your Son
  was made known by the message of an
      angel,
  may by his passion and cross
  be brought to the glory of his resurrection;
  through the same Christ our Lord.
  Amen.

ADVENT—Thursday Morning

Blessed is he who comes in the name of the Lord.
   Hosanna in the highest!
O Lord, open my lips.
   And my mouth shall declare your praise.

Canticle of Isaiah (40:1-8): God Consoles His Exiled People

Ant. I baptize you with water; he will baptize you with
   the Holy Spirit and fire. (Lk 3:17)

A voice cries, "Prepare in the wilderness
   a way for the Lord.
Make a straight highway for our God
   across the desert.

"Let every valley be filled in,
   every mountain and hill be laid low,
let every cliff become a plain,
   and the ridges a valley;
then the glory of the Lord shall be revealed
   and all mankind shall see it;
   for the mouth of the Lord has spoken."

Go upon a high mountain,
   joyful messenger to Zion,
Shout with a loud voice,
   joyful messenger to Jerusalem.
Shout without fear,
   say to the towns of Judah,
   "Here is your God."

Glory to the Father and to the Son and to the Holy
   Spirit;
   as in the beginning, so now, and for ever. Amen.

Ant. I baptize you with water; he will baptize you
   with the Holy Spirit and fire.

Collect Prayer

Let us pray (pause for silent prayer)
Father of love
you made a new creation
through Jesus Christ your Son.
May his coming free us from sin
and renew his life within us,
for he is Lord for ever and ever.
    Amen.

Reading   Mk 1:1-5

This is the Good News about Jesus Christ, the Son of God. It began as the prophet Isaiah had written: " 'Here is my messenger,' says God; 'I will send him ahead of you to open the way for you.' Someone is shouting in the desert: 'Get the Lord's road ready for him, make a straight path for him to travel! ' " So John appeared in the desert, baptizing people and preaching his message. "Turn away from your sins and be baptized," he told the people, "and God will forgive your sins." Everybody from the region of Judea and the city of Jerusalem went out to hear John. They confessed their sins and he baptized them in the Jordan river.

Response

Look up, hold your heads high.
    Your freedom is drawing near.

Canticle of Zachary   See page 255

Ant. Take courage! God himself is coming to save us.

Morning Prayer

Lord Jesus Christ,
at your first coming you sent your messenger
to prepare a way before you;
stir up the preaching of the Gospel in your Church
and turn the hearts of the disobedient to true
*   repentance*
that at your second coming to judge the world
we may be found an acceptable people in your sight;
for yours is the power and the glory for ever and ever.
  Amen.

Apostles' Creed   **Lord's Prayer**

There is only one physician,
  both carnal and spiritual, born and unborn,
  God become man, true life in death:
  sprung both from Mary and from God,
  first subject to suffering and then incapable of it
  —Jesus Christ our Lord.

                                    St. Ignatius of Antioch

The Word had life in himself.
And this life brought light to men.

Psalm 75: Judgment Belongs to God

Ant. Christ will come in glory to judge the living and
the dead.

We praise you, God, we praise you!
    We proclaim how great you are,
    and tell the wonderful things you have done!

"I have set a time for judgment," says God,
    "and I will judge with fairness.
Though the earth and all who live on it disappear,
    I will keep its foundations firm.
I tell the proud not to brag,
    and the wicked not to be arrogant;
I tell them to quit showing off,
    and to stop their bragging."

Judgment does not come from the east or from the
        west,
    from the north or from the south;
it is God who does the judging,
    putting some down and lifting others up.
The Lord holds a cup in his hand,
    full of fresh wine, very strong;
he pours it out, and all the wicked drink it;
    they drink it down to the last drop.

But I will never stop speaking of the God of Jacob,
    or singing praises to him.
He will break the power of the wicked,
    but the power of the righteous will be increased.

Glory to the Father and to the Son and to the Holy
        Spirit;
    as in the beginning, so now, and for ever. Amen.

Ant. Christ will come in glory to judge the living and the dead.

Psalm Prayer

Let us pray (pause for silent prayer)
Father,
by the passion of your Son
you proclaimed the final judgment of the world
and deposed the prince of darkness by the power of
*   the cross.*
May you shatter the pride of our hearts
and raise us to the glory of the resurrection.
We ask this through the same Christ our Lord.
   Amen.

Reading   **2 Pt 3:8-13**

Do not forget this one thing, my dear friends! There is no difference in the Lord's sight between one day and a thousand years; to him the two are the same. The Lord is not slow to do what he has promised, as some think. Instead, he is patient with you, because he does not want anyone to be destroyed, but wants all to turn away from their sins. But the Day of the Lord will come as a thief. On that Day the heavens will disappear with a shrill noise, the heavenly bodies will burn up and be destroyed, and the earth with everything in it will vanish. Since all these things will be destroyed in this way, what kind of people should you be? Your lives should be holy and dedicated to God, as you wait for the Day of God, and do your best to make it come soon—the Day when the heavens will burn up and be destroyed, and the heavenly bodies will be melted by the heat. But God has promised new heavens and a new earth, where righteousness will be at home, and we wait for these.

Response

Blessed is the womb that bore you, O Christ.
And the breasts that nursed you.

Canticle of Mary   **See page 256**

Ant. O Radiant Dawn,
           splendor of eternal light, sun of justice:
           Come, shine on those lost in the darkness of
           death.

Let Us Pray

Let us pray to Christ, the joy of all who wait for his
           coming:
      Come, Lord Jesus.
You existed before all ages and all times.
      Come and save us in this present age.
You made the world and all it contains.
      Come and save the work of your hands.
You took on our humanity, doomed to death.
      Come and save us from the power of death.
You came to bring us abundant life.
      Come and give fresh life to a fallen world.

(spontaneous prayer)

Evening Prayer

All-powerful God,
increase our strength of will for doing good
that Christ may find an eager welcome at his coming
and call us to his side in the kingdom of heaven,
where he lives and reigns with you and the Holy Spirit,
one God, for ever and ever.
      Amen.

Apostles' Creed   **Lord's Prayer**

JOHN THE BAPTIST AND FORERUNNER

There was a man sent from God
    whose name was John.
    He came to bear witness to the Light,
    to prepare an upright people for the Lord.

There is no one born of woman
    greater than John the Baptist.

God our Father,
    the voice of John the Baptist challenges us
        to repentance
    and points the way to Christ the Lord.
    Open our ears to his message,
    and free our hearts to turn from our sins
    and receive the life of the gospel.
    We ask this through Christ our Lord.
    Amen.

ADVENT—Friday Morning

Blessed is he who comes in the name of the Lord.
Hosanna in the highest!
O Lord, open my lips.
And my mouth shall declare your praise.

Canticle of Isaiah (55:1-5): The New and Everlasting Covenant

Ant. He who comes to me will never be hungry: he
who believes in me will never thirst. (Jn 6:35)

O, come to the water all you who are thirsty;
though you have no money, come!
Buy corn without money, and eat,
and at no cost, wine and milk.

Why spend money on what is not bread,
your wages on what fails to satisfy?
Listen, listen to me, and you will have good things to
eat
and rich food to enjoy.
Pay attention, come to me;
listen, and your soul will live.

With you I will make an everlasting covenant
out of the favors promised to David.
See, I have made of you a witness to the peoples,
a leader and a master of the nations.

See, you will summon a nation you never knew,
those unknown will come hurrying to you,
for the sake of the Lord your God,
of the Holy One of Israel who will glorify you.

Glory to the Father and to the Son and to the Holy
Spirit;
as in the beginning, so now, and for ever. Amen.

Ant. He who comes to me will never be hungry: he who believes in me will never thirst.

Collect Prayer

Let us pray (pause for silent prayer)
Lord Jesus,
you are the bread of life.
Teach us to live by your wisdom
and to ratify again and again the covenant of love
which you have established in your blood;
yours is the power and the glory,
now and forever.
   Amen.

Reading   **Jer 23:5-6**

See, the days are coming—it is Yahweh who speaks—when I will raise a virtuous Branch for David, who will reign as true king and be wise, practicing honesty and integrity in the land. In his days Judah will be saved and Israel dwell in confidence. And this is the name he will be called: Yahweh-our-integrity.

Response

The Lord God will make him a king.
   And his kingdom will have no end.

Canticle of Zachary   **See page 255**

Ant. Come, Lord, do not delay: Visit your people in peace.

Morning Prayer

All-powerful God,
help us to look forward in hope
to the coming of our Savior.
May we live as he has taught,
ready to welcome him with burning love and faith.
We ask this through the same Christ our Lord.
  Amen.

Apostles' Creed   **Lord's Prayer**

The Psalter is that portion of the sacred volume
  which more than any other
  both reveals and supports
  the hidden life of the servants of God
  in every age.

                    John Henry Newman

ADVENT—Friday Evening

The Word had life in himself.
And this life brought light to men.

Psalm 80: God's Vineyard

Ant. I am the real vine and my Father is the gardener.
(Jn 15:1)

Listen to us, Shepherd of Israel;
hear us, leader of your flock.
Seated on your throne on the cherubim,
reveal your love for the tribes of Ephraim,
Benjamin, and Manasseh!
Show us your strength;
come and save us!

Bring us back, God!
Show us your love, and we will be saved!

How much longer, Lord God Almighty,
will you be angry with your people's prayers?
You have given us tears to eat,
a large cup of tears to drink.
You let the neighboring nations fight over our land,
and our enemies make fun of us.

Bring us back, Almighty God!
Show us your love, and we will be saved!

You brought a grapevine out of Egypt;
you drove out other nations and planted it in their
land,
You cleared a place for it to grow;
its roots went deep, and it spread out over the whole
land.

It covered the hills with its shade,
the giant cedars with its branches.

58

It extended its branches to the Mediterranean Sea,
    and as far as the Euphrates River.
Why did you break down the fences around it?
    Now anyone passing by can steal its grapes
wild pigs trample it down,
    and all the wild animals eat it.

Turn to us, Almighty God!
    Look down from heaven at us;
    come and save your grapevine!
Come and save this vine that you yourself planted,
    this young vine you made grow so strong!

Our enemies have set it on fire and cut it down;
    look at them in anger and destroy them!
Protect and preserve the people you have chosen,
    the nation you made grow so strong!
We will never turn away from you again;
    keep us alive, and we will praise you.

Bring us back, Lord God Almighty!
    Show us your love, and we will be saved!

Glory to the Father and to the Son and to the Holy
        Spirit;
    as in the beginning, so now, and for ever. Amen.

Ant. I am the real vine and my Father is the gardener.

Psalm Prayer

Let us pray (pause for silent prayer)
Lord God, eternal Shepherd,
you have nurtured the vineyard you have planted
so that it extends over the whole world.
Help us be to your Son as branches to the vine:
that, planted firmly in your love,

we might testify before the world to your great power.
We ask this through Christ Jesus our Lord.
Amen.

Reading   1 Thes 5:16-24

Be joyful always, pray at all times, be thankful in all
circumstances. This is what God wants of you, in your
life in Christ Jesus. Do not restrain the Holy Spirit; do
not despise inspired messages. Put all things to the
test: keep what is good, and avoid every kind of evil.
May the God who gives us peace make you completely
his, and keep your whole being, spirit, soul, and body,
free from all fault, at the coming of our Lord Jesus
Christ. He who calls you will do it, for he is faithful!

Response

The Holy Spirit will overshadow you, O Virgin Mary.
And the holy child will be called the Son of God.

Canticle of Mary   See page 256

Ant. O King of all the nations,
      the only joy of every human heart;
      O Keystone of the mighty arch of man:
      Come and save the creature you fashioned from
        the dust.

Let Us Pray

Let us pray to the eternal Word, who shows us a new
    and living way to the heavenly sanctuary:
    Come and save us.
In God we live and move and have our being.
    Come and show us we are his people.
You are not far from any one of us.
    Reveal yourself to all who seek you.

Father of the poor and comforter of the afflicted,
   Set captives free and give joy to the sorrowful.
You hate death and love life.
   Free us from eternal death.

(spontaneous prayer)

Evening Prayer

God of mercy and consolation,
help us in our weakness and free us from sin.
Hear our prayers
that we may rejoice at the coming of your Son,
who lives and reigns with you and the Holy Spirit,
one God, for ever and ever.
   Amen.

Apostles' Creed   **Lord's Prayer**

We may not look at our pleasure
   to go to heaven in feather beds:
   It is not the way,
   for our Lord himself went thither with great pain
      and by many tribulations,
   which was the path wherein he walked thither,
   for the servant may not look to be in better case
      than his master.
                                    St. Thomas More

TO JOSEPH OUR PROTECTOR

Joseph, son of David,
  do not be afraid to take Mary, your wife,
    into your own home.
  She will give birth to a Son
  and you shall call him Jesus,
  for he shall save his people from their sins.

Joseph did as the angel of the Lord
    commanded him,
  and received her into his home.

Father,
  you entrusted our Savior to the care of St.
    Joseph.
  By the help of his prayers
  may your Church continue to serve its Lord,
    Jesus Christ,
  who lives and reigns with you and the Holy
    Spirit,
  one God, for ever and ever.
  Amen.

ADVENT—Saturday Morning

Blessed is he who comes in the name of the Lord.
  Hosanna in the highest!
O Lord, open my lips.
  And my mouth shall declare your praise.

Canticle of Micah (5:1-5): Bethlehem, Birthplace of the Messiah

Ant. The Virgin will give birth to a Son and they will
  call him Emmanuel. (Mt 1:23)

You, Bethlehem Ephrathah,
  the least of the clans of Judah,
out of you will be born for me
  the one who is to rule over Israel;
his origin goes back to the distant past,
  to the days of old.

The Lord is therefore going to abandon them
  till the time when she who is to give birth gives birth.
Then the remnant of his brothers will come back
  to the sons of Israel.

He will stand and feed his flock
  with the power of the Lord,
  with the majesty of the name of his God.
They will live secure, for from then on
  he will extend his power to the ends of the land.
  He himself will be peace.

Glory to the Father and to the Son and to the Holy
    Spirit;
  as in the beginning, so now, and for ever. Amen.

Ant. The Virgin will give birth to a Son and they will
  call him Emmanuel.

Collect Prayer

Let us pray (pause for silent prayer)
God of love and mercy,
help us to follow the example of Mary,
always ready to do your will.
At the message of an angel
she welcomed your eternal Son
and filled with the light of your Spirit,
she became the temple of your Word,
who lives and reigns with you and the Holy Spirit,
one God, for ever and ever.
  Amen.

Reading

Mt 1:18-23

This was the way that Jesus Christ was born. His mother Mary was engaged to Joseph, but before they were married she found out that she was going to have a baby by the Holy Spirit. Joseph, to whom she was engaged, was a man who always did what was right; but he did not want to disgrace Mary publicly, so he made plans to break the engagement secretly. While he was thinking about all this, an angel of the Lord appeared to him in a dream and said: "Joseph, descendant of David, do not be afraid to take Mary to be your wife. For it is by the Holy Spirit that she has conceived. She will give birth to a son and you will name him Jesus—for he will save his people from their sins." Now all this happened in order to make come true what the Lord had said through the prophet: "The virgin will become pregnant and give birth to a son, and he will be called Emmanuel" (which means, "God is with us").

Response

Our God comes, born as man of David's line,
   Enthroned as king for ever, alleluia.

Canticle of Zachary   **See page 255**

Ant. Like the sun in the morning sky,
      the Savior of the world will dawn;
      like rain on the meadows he will descend.

Morning Prayer

Father, all-powerful God,
the mystery of your eternal Word
took flesh on our earth
when the Virgin Mary placed her life
at the service of your plan.
Lift our minds in watchful hope
to hear the voice which announces his glory
and open our minds to receive the Spirit
who prepares for his coming.
We ask this through Christ our Lord.
   Amen.

Apostles' Creed   **Lord's Prayer**

**When you use psalms and hymns in prayer
   hold in your heart what you say with your voice.**
                                    St. Augustine of Hippo

ADVENT—Saturday Evening

The Word had life in himself.
And this life brought light to men.

Psalm 122: Jerusalem, our Mother

Ant. You have come to the city of the living God, the
heavenly Jerusalem. (Heb 12:22)

I was glad when they said to me,
"Let us go to the Lord's house!"
And now we are here,
standing inside the gates of Jerusalem!

Jerusalem is a city restored
in beautiful order and harmony!
This is where the tribes come,
the tribes of Israel,
to give thanks to the Lord,
as he commanded them.
This is where the law courts are,
where the king judges his people.

Pray for the peace of Jerusalem!
"May those who love you prosper!
May there be peace inside your walls,
and safety in your palaces."
For the sake of my friends and companions,
I say to Jerusalem, "Peace be with you!"
For the sake of the house of the Lord, our God,
I pray for your prosperity.

Glory to the Father and to the Son and to the Holy
Spirit;
as in the beginning, so now, and for ever. Amen.

Ant. You have come to the city of the living God, the
heavenly Jerusalem.

Psalm Prayer

Let us pray (pause for silent prayer)
Lord Jesus Christ, Son of the living God,
by love's decree you came and lived among us
to establish a community of faith and fellowship;
gather all nations and peoples into your Church
and make it the city of peace and justice,
a model of the heavenly Jerusalem;
for yours is the power and the glory for ever and ever.
   Amen.

Reading   Lk 1:26-33, 38

In the sixth month of Elizabeth's pregnancy God sent
the angel Gabriel to a town in Galilee named Nazareth.
He had a message for a girl promised in marriage to a
man named Joseph, who was a descendant of King
David. The girl's name was Mary. The angel came
to her and said, "Peace be with you! The Lord is with
you, and has greatly blessed you!" Mary was deeply
troubled by the angel's message, and she wondered
what his words meant. The angel said to her: "Don't
be afraid, Mary, for God has been gracious to you.
You will become pregnant and give birth to a son, and
you will name him Jesus. He will be great and will
be called the Son of the Most High God. The Lord
God will make him a king, as his ancestor David was,
and he will be the king of the descendants of Jacob
for ever; his kingdom will never end!" "I am the
Lord's servant," said Mary; "may it happen to me as
you have said." And the angel left her.

Response

Blessed are you among women, alleluia.
   And blessed is the fruit of your womb, alleluia.

Canticle of Mary   See page 256

Ant. O Emmanuel,
    God who lives with us to rule and guide,
    the nations of the earth cry out in longing:
    Come and set us free, our Savior God.

Let Us Pray

Let us pray to Jesus Christ, Son of God and Son of
    Mary:
  O Savior, save us.
Incarnate Savior, true God and true man,
  O Savior, save us.
God from God and Light from Light,
  O Savior, save us.
Judge of the living and the dead,
  O Savior, save us.
Your kingdom will have no end.
  O Savior, save us.

(spontaneous prayer)

Evening Prayer

God of love and mercy,
help us to follow the example of Mary,
always ready to do your will.
At the message of an angel
she welcomed your eternal Son
and, filled with the light of your Spirit,
she became the temple of your Word,
who lives and reigns with you and the Holy Spirit,
one God, for ever and ever.
  Amen.

Apostles' Creed   Lord's Prayer

ADVENT CANTICLE TO MARY

Mother of our Lord and Savior,
  pathway to God's kingdom,
  gate of heaven,
  bright star of the sea:

Aid your fallen people,
  as we struggle to rise once again.

Nature stood in wonder,
  as you became Mother
  of Jesus Christ your Creator.

Virgin you were before the Lord's birth,
  as Gabriel greeted you,
  and virgin you remained:
  ask God's mercy on us sinners.

Holy Mother of God, you brought forth the
      Child
  whom the whole world cannot contain.

O God our Father,
  by the fruitful virginity of the Blessed Virgin
      Mary
  you conferred the benefits of everlasting
      salvation upon all mankind;
  grant that we may feel the power of her
      intercession,
  through whom we received the Author of
      Life,
  Jesus Christ our Lord.
  Amen.

Christmas Eve

Bethlehem, make ready, for Eden has been opened for
    all;
   Ephratha, be alert, for the Tree of Life has blossomed
    forth from the Virgin in the cave.
Her womb has become a spiritual paradise
   wherein the divine Fruit was planted;
if we eat of it, we shall live and not die like Adam.
Christ is coming forth to bring back to life
   the likeness that had been lost in the beginning.

Byzantine Liturgy

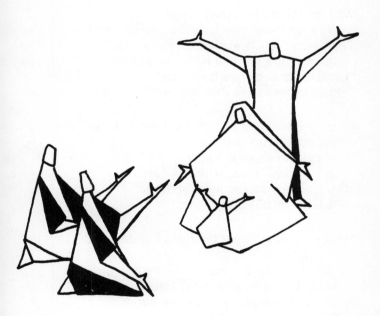

CHRISTMASTIDE

Glory to God in the highest, alleluia.
And peace to his people on earth, alleluia.
O Lord, open my lips.
And my mouth shall declare your praise.

Psalm 2: God's Chosen Son, our Messianic King

Ant.   The angel said to the shepherds: Today a Savior
has been born to you, the Messiah and Lord.
(Lk 2:11)

Why do the nations plan rebellion?
Why do these people make useless plots?
Their kings revolt, their rulers plot together
against the Lord and his chosen king.
"Let us free ourselves from their rule," they say;
"Let us throw off their control."

From his throne in heaven the Lord laughs
and makes fun of them.
He speaks to them in anger,
and terrifies them with his fury.
"On Zion, my sacred hill," he says,
"I have installed my king."

"I will announce what the Lord has declared," says the
king.
"The Lord said to me: 'You are my son;
today I have become your father.
Ask, and I will give you all the nations;
the whole earth will be yours.
You will rule over them with an iron hand;
you will break them in pieces like a clay pot.' "

Now listen to me, you kings;
pay attention, you rulers!

Serve the Lord with fear;
   tremble and bow down to him;
or else he will be angry, and you will die
   for his anger is quickly aroused.
    Happy are all who go to him for protection!

Glory to the Father and to the Son and to the Holy
    Spirit;
   as in the beginning, so now, and for ever. Amen.

Ant. The angel said to the shepherds: Today a Savior
    has been born to you, the Messiah and Lord.

Psalm Prayer

Let us pray (pause for silent prayer)
God of power and life,
glory of all who believe in you,
fill the world with your splendor
and show the nations the light of your truth.
We ask this through Jesus our Lord.
  Amen.

Reading   Heb 1:1-3

In the past God spoke to our ancestors many times
and in many ways through the prophets, but in these
last days he has spoken to us through his Son. He is
the one through whom God created the universe, the
one whom God has chosen to possess all things at the
end. He shines with the brightness of God's glory; he
is the exact likeness of God's own being, and sustains
the universe with his powerful word. After he had
made men clean from their sins, he sat down in heaven
at the right side of God, the Supreme Power.

73

Response

The Lord has made known his salvation, alleluia.
To all the ends of the earth, alleluia.

Canticle of Zachary   **See page 255**

Ant. Glory to God in the highest
     and peace to his people on earth, alleluia. (Lk
     2:14)

Morning Prayer

Lord God,
we praise you for creating the human race
and still more for restoring it in Christ.
Your Son shared our weakness;
may we share his glory,
for he lives and reigns with you and the Holy Spirit,
one God, for ever and ever.
   Amen.

Apostles' Creed   **Lord's Prayer**

**The Son of God became the Son of Man
   so that the sons of men could become
   the sons of God.**

                                   St. Augustine of Hippo

Jesus Christ is the true light.
That illumines every person coming into this world.

Psalm 110: The Messianic King, Priest and Conqueror

Ant. I bring you good news of great joy: A Savior is
born for you today. (Lk 2:11)

The Lord said to my Lord, the king,
"Sit here at my right side,
until I put your enemies under your feet."

From Zion the Lord will extend your royal power.
"Rule over your enemies," he says.
The day you fight your enemies
your people will volunteer.
Like the dew early in the morning,
your young men will come to you on the sacred hills.

The Lord made a solemn promise and will not take it
back:
"You will be a priest forever,
in the priestly order of Melchizedek."

The Lord is at your right side:
he will defeat kings on the day he becomes angry.
The king will drink from the stream by the road,
and strengthened, he will stand victorious.

Glory to the Father and to the Son and to the Holy
Spirit;
as in the beginning, so now, and for ever. Amen.

Ant. I bring you good news of great joy: A Savior is
born for you today.

Psalm Prayer

Let us pray (pause for silent prayer)
Lord Jesus Christ,
your birth is the joy of the whole world
as you come to do the will of him who sent you;
be our high priest for ever,
strengthen your Church against its enemies,
and quench our thirst for things eternal
  with the fresh streams of your Spirit;
for yours is the power and the glory for ever and ever.
Amen.

Reading   1 Jn 1:1-3

We write to you about the Word of life, which has existed from the very beginning: we have heard it, and we have seen it with our eyes; yes, we have seen it, and our hands have touched it. When this life became visible, we saw it; so we speak of it and tell you about the eternal life which was with the Father and was made known to us. What we have seen and heard we tell to you also, so that you will join with us in the fellowship that we have with the Father and with his Son Jesus Christ.

Response

The Word was made flesh, alleluia.
And lived among us, alleluia.

Canticle of Mary   See page 256

Ant. Today Christ is born; today the Savior has ap-
          peared;
        today the angels are singing on earth,
            the archangels are rejoicing;
        today the saints exult and say:
        Glory to God in the highest, alleluia.

Let Us Pray

You, Christ, are the king of glory,
   Eternal Son of the Father.
When you became man to set us free
   You did not disdain the virgin's womb.
You overcame the sting of death
   And opened the kingdom of heaven to all believers.
You are seated at God's right hand in glory.
   We believe that you will come and be our judge.
Come, then, Lord sustain your people,
   Bought with the price of your own blood,
And bring us with your saints.
   To everlasting glory.

(*spontaneous prayer*)

Evening Prayer

All-powerful and unseen God,
the coming of your light into our world
has made the darkness vanish.
Teach us to proclaim the birth of your Son Jesus Christ,
who lives and reigns with you and the Holy Spirit,
one God, for ever and ever.
   Amen.

Apostles' Creed   **Lord's Prayer**

In giving us his Son, God gave us everything.
   By delivering up to us his unique Word,
   he revealed everything to us.
   There is nothing further to wait for after Jesus Christ.
                                        St. John of the Cross

AN ANCIENT SALUTATION TO THE
BLESSED VIRGIN MARY

Rejoice, sing for joy, exult,
  O Mary, so highly favored.
  The Lord is with you.
Blessed indeed among women,
  and blessed, blessed, blessed
    is the fruit of your womb,
  Christ Jesus.
Maiden—Mother of our Lord,
  pray the Father, that we mortals
  increase in the Holy Spirit,
  and grow up in the Son
into the fullness of the stature of the children
  of God.

FEAST OF THE HOLY FAMILY—Morning
(First Sunday after Christmas)

Glory to God in the highest, alleluia.
   And peace to his people on earth, alleluia.
O Lord, open my lips.
   And my mouth shall declare your praise.

Psalm 127: The Happy Home at Nazareth

Ant. The shepherds came in haste and found Mary
   and Joseph, and the Baby lying in a manger. (Lk
   2:16)

If the Lord does not build the house,
   the work of the builders is useless;
if the Lord does not protect the city,
   it does no good for the sentries to stand guard.
It is useless to work so hard for a living,
   getting up early and going to bed late,
   because the Lord gives rest to those he loves.

Children are a gift from the Lord;
   they are a real blessing.
The sons a man has when he is young
   are like arrows in a soldier's hand.
Happy is the man who has many such arrows!
   He will never be defeated
   when he meets his enemies in the place of judgment.

Glory to the Father and to the Son and to the Holy
      Spirit;
   as in the beginning, so now, and for ever. **Amen.**

Ant. The shepherds came in haste and found Mary
   and Joseph, and the Baby lying in a manger.

Psalm Prayer

Let us pray (pause for silent prayer)
Father,
help us to live as the holy family,
united in respect and love.
Bring us to the joy and peace of your eternal home.
We ask this through Christ our Lord.
   Amen.

Reading   **Dt 6:4-7**

Hear, O Israel: Yahweh is our God, Yahweh alone;
and you shall love the Lord your God with all your
heart and with all your soul and with all your might.
And these words which I command you this day shall
be upon your heart; and you shall teach them diligently
to your children, and you shall talk of them when you
sit in your house, and when you walk by the way, and
when you lie down, and when you rise.

Response

Jesus went down with them to Nazareth.
   And lived in subjection to them.

Canticle of Zachary   **See page 255**

Ant. The Child grew and became strong;
      he was full of wisdom
      and God's blessings were with him. (Lk 2:40)

Morning Prayer

Eternal Father,
we want to live as Jesus, Mary and Joseph,
in peace with you and with one another.
May the example of the holy family
strengthen us to face the troubles of life.
Grant this through Christ our Lord.
  Amen.

Apostles' Creed   **Lord's Prayer**

In adoring the birth of our Savior,
  we find that we are celebrating the commencement
    of our own life.
  For the birth of Christ is the source of life
    for the Christian people
  and the birthday of the Head is the birthday of the
    body.

St. Leo the Great

Jesus Christ is the true light,
That illumines every person coming into this world.

Psalm 113: Praise the Lord of Children

Ant. Joseph was the husband of Mary and of her was
born Jesus, who is called the Christ. (Mt 1:16)

You servants of the Lord,
   praise his name!
His name will be praised,
   now and forever!

From the east to the west,
   the Lord's name be praised!
The Lord rules over all nations,
   his glory is above the heavens.

There is no one like the Lord our God;
   he lives in the heights above,
but he bends down
   to see the heavens and the earth.

He raises the poor from the dust;
   he lifts the needy from their misery,
and makes them companions of princes,
   the princes of his people.
He honors the childless wife in her home;
   he makes her happy by giving her children.

Glory to the Father and to the Son and to the Holy
      Spirit;
   as in the beginning, so now, and for ever. Amen.

Ant. Joseph was the husband of Mary and of her was
born Jesus, who is called the Christ.

Psalm Prayer

Let us pray (pause for silent prayer)
May your name be praised,
Lord our God,
from the rising to the setting of the sun,
and through the prayers of Mary and Joseph
unite our families in peace and love.
We ask this in the name of Jesus the Lord.
   Amen.

Reading   Col 3:12-14, 17

You are the people of God; he loved you and chose
you for his own. Therefore, you must put on compassion, kindness, humility, gentleness, and patience.
Be helpful to one another, and forgive one another,
whenever any of you has a complaint against someone
else. You must forgive each other in the same way
that the Lord has forgiven you. And to all these add
love, which binds all things together in perfect unity.
Everything you do or say, then, should be done in the
name of the Lord Jesus, as you give thanks through
him to God the Father.

Response

The Word was made flesh, alleluia.
   And lived among us, alleluia.

Canticle of Mary   See page 256

Ant. His mother treasured all these things in her heart.
   (Lk 2:51)

83

Let Us Pray

Lord Jesus Christ, Son of the living God,
  Make us holy.
Word made flesh for our salvation,
  Make us holy.
By the mystery of your subjection to Mary and Joseph,
  Make us holy.
By the mystery of your daily work and prayer at
  Nazareth,
  Make us holy.
By your example of love and service,
  Make us holy.
By your growing in wisdom, age and grace before God
  and men,
  Make us holy.

(spontaneous prayer)

Evening Prayer

Father in heaven, creator of all,
you ordered the earth to bring forth life
and crowned its goodness by creating the
  family of man.
In history's moment when all was ready,
you sent your Son to dwell in time,
obedient to the laws of life in our world.
Teach us the sanctity of human love,
show us the value of family life,
and help us to live in peace with our neighbors
that we may share in your life for ever.
We ask this through Christ our Lord.
  Amen.

Apostles' Creed   **Lord's Prayer**

FOR FAMILIES

O God our Father,
bind together in your all-embracing love
   every family on earth.
Banish anger and bitterness within them;
nourish forgiveness and peace.
Bestow upon parents such wisdom and
   patience
that they may gently exercise the disciplines
   of love,
and call forth from their children
   their greatest virtue and their highest skill.
Instill in children such independence and
   self-respect
that they may freely obey their parents,
and grow in the joys of companionship.
Open ears to hear the truth within the words
   another speaks;
open eyes to see the reality beneath another's
   appearance;
and make the mutual affection of families
   a sign of your kingdom;
through Jesus Christ our Lord.
Amen.

CHRISTMAS
Morning—Jan. 1 - The Epiphany

Come, let us adore the Word made flesh, alleluia.
The Son of the living God, alleluia.
O Lord, open my lips.
And my mouth shall declare your praise.

Psalm 45: The Marriage of the Messianic King

Ant. Christ loved the Church and gave his life for it.
(Eph 5:25)

You are the most handsome of all men;
   you are an eloquent speaker;
   God has always blessed you!
Buckle on your sword, mighty king;
   you are powerful and majestic!

Ride on in majesty to victory,
   for the defense of truth and justice!
   Your strength will win you great victories!
Your arrows are sharp and pierce the hearts of your
      enemies;
   nations fall down at your feet.

The throne that God has given you
   will last forever and ever!
You rule over your kingdom with justice;
   you love what is right and hate what is evil.
That is why God, your God, has chosen you,
   and has poured out more happiness on you
   than on anyone else.
The perfume of myrrh, aloes, and cassia is on your
      clothes;
   musicians entertain you in ivory palaces.
Among the ladies of your court are daughters of kings,
   and at the right of your throne stands the queen,
   wearing ornaments of finest gold.

Bride of the king, listen to what I say—
   forget your people and your relatives.
Your beauty will make the king desire you;
   He is your master, so you must obey him.
The people of Tyre will bring you gifts;
   rich people will try to win your favor.

The princess is in the palace—how beautiful she is!
   Her gown is made of gold thread.
In her colorful gown she is led to the king,
   followed by her bridesmaids,
   and they also are brought to him.
With joy and gladness they come
   and enter the king's palace.

You, my king, will have many sons
   to take the place of your ancestors,
   and you will make them rulers over the whole earth.
My song will keep your fame alive forever,
   and everyone will praise you for all time to come.

Glory to the Father and to the Son and to the Holy
    Spirit;
   as in the beginning, so now, and for ever. Amen.

Ant. Christ loved the Church and gave his life for it.

Psalm Prayer

Let us pray (pause for silent prayer)
When you took on flesh, Lord Jesus,
you made a marriage of mankind with God.
Help us to be faithful to your word
and endure our exile bravely
until we are called to the heavenly marriage feast:
to which the Virgin Mary, exemplar of your Church,
has preceded us;
yours is the power and the glory for ever and ever.
  Amen.

Reading   **Mi 5:1-4**

You Bethlehem-Ephrathah, the least of the clans of
Judah, out of you will be born for me the one who is
to rule over Israel; his origin goes back to the distant
past, to the days of old. Yahweh is therefore going to
abandon them till the time when she who is to give
birth gives birth. Then the remnant of his brothers will
come back to the sons of Israel. He will stand and
feed his flock with the power of Yahweh, with the
majesty of the name of his God.

Response

Here is a mystery beyond all telling:
   The womb of the virgin becomes the temple of God.

Canticle of Zachary   See page 255

Ant. O wondrous exchange!
         The Creator of the human race,
         having assumed a living body,
         was born of the Virgin,
         and becoming man without man's aid,
         enriched us with his divinity.

Morning Prayer

God our Father,
may we always have the prayers
of the Virgin Mother Mary,
for through Jesus Christ her Son
you bring us light and salvation,
for he lives and reigns with you and the Holy Spirit,
one God, for ever and ever.
   Amen.

Apostles' Creed   **Lord's Prayer**

CHRISTMAS
Evening—Jan. 1 - The Epiphany

Christ, the light of the world, is born for us.
Come, let us adore him, alleluia.

Psalm 46: His Delight Is to Be With the Children of Men

Ant. He shall be called Emmanuel: God-is-with-us.
(Mt 1:23)

God is our shelter and strength,
    always ready to help in times of trouble.
So we will not be afraid, even if the earth is shaken
    and mountains fall into the ocean depths;
even if the seas roar and rage,
    and the hills are shaken by the violence.
The Lord Almighty is with us;
    the God of Jacob is our refuge!

There is a river that brings joy to the city of God,
    to the sacred house of the Most High.
God lives in the city, and it will never be destroyed;
    at early dawn he will come to its help.
Nations are terrified, kingdoms are shaken;
    God roars out and the earth dissolves.
The Lord Almighty is with us;
    the God of Jacob is our refuge!

Come, see what the Lord has done!
    See what amazing things he has done on earth!
He stops wars all over the world;
    he breaks bows, destroys spears,
    and sets shields on fire!
He says, "Stop your fighting and know that I am God,
    supreme among the nations, supreme over the
        world!"
The Lord Almighty is with us;
    the God of Jacob is our refuge!

Glory to the Father and to the Son and to the Holy
   Spirit;
   as in the beginning, so now, and for ever. Amen.

Ant. He shall be called Emmanuel: God-is-with-us.

Psalm Prayer

Let us pray (pause for silent prayer)
God our Father,
you chose the Blessed Virgin Mary
to become the mother of our Savior;
grant that we who call to mind
   her great faith and love
may in all things seek to do your will
and always rejoice in your salvation.
We ask this through Jesus Christ our Lord
   Amen.

Reading   **Gal 4:3-7**

We too were slaves of the ruling spirits of the universe,
before we reached spiritual maturity. But when the
right time finally came, God sent his own Son. He
came as the son of a human mother, and lived under
the Jewish Law, to set free those who were under the
Law, so that we might become God's sons. To show
that you are his sons, God sent the Spirit of his Son
into our hearts, the Spirit who cries, "Father, my
Father." So then, you are no longer a slave, but a son.
And since you are his son, God will give you all he
has for his sons.

Response

The Word was made flesh, alleluia.
   And lived among us, alleluia.

Canticle of Mary   **See page 256**

Ant. Blessed is the womb that bore you, O Christ,
and blessed are the breasts that nursed you,
the Lord and Savior of the world, alleluia.

Let Us Pray

Jesus, Son of the living God, splendor of the Father,
eternal light,
Have mercy on us.
Jesus, king of glory, sun of justice, son of the Virgin
Mary,
Have mercy on us.
Jesus, wonder-counselor, mighty God, father of the
world to come,
Have mercy on us.
Jesus, prince of peace, source of life, exemplar of
holiness,
Have mercy on us.
Jesus, lover of mankind, father of the poor, treasure
of the faithful,
Have mercy on us.
Jesus, good shepherd, inexhaustible wisdom, our way
and our life,
Have mercy on us.
Jesus, joy of angels and crown of all the saints,
Have mercy on us.

(spontaneous prayer)

Evening Prayer

Father of our Lord Jesus Christ,
our glory is to stand before the world
as your own sons and daughters.
May the simple beauty of Jesus' birth

summon us always to love what is most deeply human,
and to see your Word made flesh
reflected in those whose lives we touch.
We ask this through Christ our Lord.
   Amen.

Apostles' Creed   **Lord's Prayer**

Learn, O Christian, how great you are,
   for you have become a sharer in the divine nature,
   and do not return to your former base condition
   by behavior unworthy of your dignity.
Remember the Head and the Body of which you are a
   member.

St. Leo the Great

PRAYER TO THE MOTHER OF GOD

Blessed are you, Mary:
in you the prophecies are fulfilled
and the dark sayings of the prophets explained.
  Moses foretold you by the burning bush and
    the cloud,
  Jacob by the ladder leading to heaven,
  David by the ark of the covenant,
  Ezechiel by the door that was closed and
    sealed.
And now in Christ's birth their mysterious
  words are made plain.
Glory to the Father who sent his only Son to
  manifest himself through Mary,
To free us from error and make her memory
  glorious in heaven and on earth.

Balai of Aleppo

THE EPIPHANY OF OUR LORD JESUS CHRIST

Where this feast is kept as a holy day of obligation it is celebrated on Jan. 6; elsewhere it is observed on the Sunday that falls between Jan. 2 and Jan. 8.

THE EPIPHANY—Morning

The Lord has shown forth his glory:
Come, let us adore him, alleluia.
O Lord, open my lips.
And my mouth shall declare your praise.

A Pauline Canticle 1 Tm 3:16: The Manifestation of Christ

Ant. Praise the Lord, all nations! Praise him, all peoples!

Jesus Christ appeared in human form,
    was shown to be right by the Spirit,
        and was seen by angels.

Ant. Praise the Lord, all nations! Praise him, all peoples!

He was preached among the nations,
    was believed in the world,
        and was taken up to heaven.

Ant. Praise the Lord, all nations! Praise him, all peoples!

He is the blessed and only Ruler,
    the King of kings and the Lord of lords.
        He alone is immortal.

Ant. Praise the Lord, all nations! Praise him, all peoples!

94

Collect Prayer

Let us pray (pause for silent prayer)
Lord God,
let the light of your glory shine within us,
and lead us through the darkness of this world
to the radiant joy of our eternal home.
We ask this through Christ our Lord.
  Amen.

Reading   Is 52:7-10

How beautiful on the mountains, are the feet of one
who brings good news, who heralds peace, brings
happiness, proclaims salvation, and tells Zion, "Your
God is king!" Listen! Your watchmen raise their
voices, they shout for joy together, for they see
Yahweh face to face, as he returns to Zion. Break
into shouts of joy together, you ruins of Jerusalem;
for Yahweh is consoling his people, redeeming Jerusalem. Yahweh bares his holy arm in the sight of all
the nations and all the ends of the earth shall see the
salvation of our God.

Response

All the kings of the earth shall adore him, alleluia.
  All the nations shall serve him, alleluia.

Canticle of Zachary   **See page 255**

Ant. Today the Church is joined to her heavenly
      Bridegroom:
      Christ washes away her sins in the Jordan;
      the Magi hasten with gifts to the royal wedding;
      and the guests are gladdened by water made
      wine, alleluia.

Morning Prayer

Father,
you revealed your Son to the nations
by the guidance of a star.
Lead us to your glory in heaven
by the light of faith.
We ask this through the same Christ our Lord.
  Amen.

Apostles' Creed   **Lord's Prayer**

The Magi bear witness by mystical gifts to belief
    not disbelief:
  with incense, they bear witness to God;
  with gold, to a king;
  with myrrh, to the one who must suffer death.
                                        St. Peter Chrysologus

THE EPIPHANY—Evening

We have seen his star in the East.
And have come to adore the Lord.

Psalm 72: Christ Reigns With Justice, Love and Peace

Ant. Seeing the Child with Mary his mother, the Magi
knelt down and worshiped him. (Mt 2:11)

Teach the king to judge with your righteousness, God,
  share with him your own justice,
so that he will rule over your people with justice,
  and govern the poor with righteousness.
May the land enjoy prosperity;
  may it experience righteousness.
May the king judge the poor fairly;
  may he help the needy and defeat the oppressors!
May your people worship you as long as the sun shines,
  as long as the moon gives light, for all time.

May the king be like rain on the fields,
  like showers falling on the land.
May righteousness flourish in his lifetime,
  and prosperity last as long as the moon shines.

His kingdom will reach from sea to sea,
  from the Euphrates River to the ends of the earth.
The peoples of the desert will bow down before him;
  his enemies will lie flat in the dust.
The kings of Spain and of the islands will offer him
    gifts;
  the kings of Arabia and Ethiopia will bring him
    offerings.
All the kings will bow down before him;
  all nations will serve him!

He rescues the poor who call to him,
    and those who are needy and neglected.
He has pity on the weak and poor;
    he saves the lives of those in need.
He rescues them from oppression and violence;
    their lives are precious to him.

Long live the king!
    May he be given gold from Arabia;
May prayers be said for him at all times;
    may God's blessings be on him always!
May there be plenty of grain in the land;
    may the hills be covered with crops,
    as fruitful as those of Lebanon.
May the cities be filled with people,
    like grass growing in the fields.

May his name never be forgotten;
    may his fame last as long as the sun.
May all nations praise him,
    may all people ask God to bless them
    as he has blessed the king.

Glory to the Father and to the Son and to the Holy
    Spirit;
    as in the beginning, so now, and for ever. Amen.

Ant. Seeing the Child with Mary his mother, the Magi
    knelt down and worshiped him.

Psalm Prayer

Let us pray (pause for silent prayer)
Almighty God,
you gave the kingdom of justice and peace
to David and his descendant,
our Lord Jesus Christ.

Extend this kingdom to every family of nations
so that through your Son,
all men might obtain true peace,
the poor receive justice,
the destitute relief,
and the people of the earth find a blessing in his name.
We ask this through the same Christ our Lord.
  Amen.

Reading   Ti 3:4-5

When the kindness and love of God our Savior appeared, he saved us. It was not because of any good works that we ourselves had done, but because of his own mercy that he saved us through the washing by which the Holy Spirit gives us new birth and new life.

Response

The Magi opened their treasures and offered him
      presents:
  Gold, frankincense and myrrh.

Canticle of Mary   See page 256

Ant. This is a holy day adorned with three mysteries:
      Today a star leads the Magi to the manger;
      Today water is made wine at the wedding;
      Today Christ is baptized by John in the Jordan
         so as to save us, alleluia.

Let Us Pray

By the wondrous birth in time of the timeless Son of
      God, let us pray to the Lord.
  Lord, have mercy.
By the humble nativity of the King of glory in the cave
      of Bethlehem, let us pray to the Lord.

Lord, have mercy.
By the splendid manifestation of the King of the Jews
to the shepherds and the Magi, let us pray to the
Lord.
Lord, have mercy.
By the spotless baptism of the beloved Son of God by
John in the Jordan, let us pray to the Lord.
Lord, have mercy.
By the revealing miracle of the water made wine at
Cana of Galilee, let us pray to the Lord.
Lord, have mercy.
For the conversion of the whole human race to our
Lord and Savior Jesus Christ, let us pray to the
Lord.
Lord, have mercy.

(spontaneous prayer)

Evening Prayer

Father of light, unchanging God,
you reveal to men of faith
the resplendent fact of the Word made flesh.
Your light is strong, your love is near;
draw us beyond the limits which this world imposes,
to the life where the Spirit makes all life complete.
We ask this through Christ our Lord.
　　Amen.

Apostles' Creed　　　　　　　　　　**Lord's Prayer**

*The above forms of morning and evening prayer may also be
used on the days that intervene between the solemnity of the
Epiphany and the feast of our Lord's Baptism.*

DOXOLOGY

To God the Father,
who loved us and made us accepted in the
    Beloved:
To God the Son,
who loved us and loosed us from our sins by
    his own blood:
To God the Holy Spirit,
who sheds the love of God abroad in our
    hearts:
To the one true God,
be all love and all glory for time and for
    eternity.
Amen.

Bishop Thomas Ken

THE BAPTISM OF OUR LORD JESUS CHRIST
(Third Sunday after Christmas)

Morning

Come, let us adore the beloved Son of God.
In whom the Father is well pleased.
O Lord, open my lips.
And my mouth shall declare your praise.

A Canticle of Isaiah (42:1-8): The Beloved Servant of God

Ant. This is my own dear Son, with whom I am well
pleased. (Mt 3:17)

Here is my servant whom I uphold,
my chosen one in whom my soul delights.
I have endowed him with my Spirit
that he may bring true justice to the nations.

He does not cry out or shout aloud,
or make his voice heard in the streets.
He does not break the crushed reed,
nor quench the wavering flame.
Faithfully he brings true justice;
he will neither waver nor be crushed
until true justice is established on earth,
for the islands are awaiting his law.

I, Yahweh, have called you to serve the cause of right;
I have taken you by the hand and formed you;
I have appointed you as a covenant of the people
and light of the nations,
to open the eyes of the blind
to free captives from prison
and those who live in darkness from the dungeon.

Glory to the Father and to the Son and to the Holy Spirit;
  as in the beginning, so now, and for ever. Amen.

Ant. This is my own dear Son, with whom I am well pleased.

Collect Prayer

Let us pray (pause for silent prayer)
Lord Jesus Christ,
you humbled yourself and received baptism at the hands of John your forerunner
and were proclaimed God's own dear Son;
grant that we who have been baptized into you
may rejoice in our divine adoption
and show ourselves the servants of all;
for yours is the power and the glory now and for ever.
  Amen.

Reading Is 61:1-2[a]

The spirit of the Lord Yahweh has been given to me, for Yahweh has anointed me. He has sent me to bring good news to the poor, to bind up hearts that are broken; to proclaim liberty to captives, freedom to those in prison; to proclaim a year of favor from Yahweh.

Response

As soon as Jesus came up out of the water,
  The Spirit came down on him like a dove.

Canticle of Zachary **See page 255**

Ant. At your baptism in the River Jordan, O Christ, the mystery of the Holy Trinity was revealed to us.

Morning Prayer

Almighty, eternal God,
when the Spirit descended upon Jesus
at his baptism in the Jordan,
you revealed him as your own beloved Son.
Keep us, your children born of water and the Spirit,
faithful to our calling.
We ask this through the same Christ our Lord.
  Amen.

Apostles' Creed **Lord's Prayer**

From the moment the Savior is washed,
  all the waters become pure for our baptism;
  the source is purified so that those who follow after
  may obtain grace.
Christ steps forward first to baptism,
  so that all Christian people may follow him
    without hesitation.
                            St. Maximus of Turin

THE BAPTISM OF OUR LORD—Evening

Christ, the light of the world, has appeared to us:
Come, let us adore him.

Psalm 29: The Lord of the Waters

Ant. Today the heavens are opened and the voice of
the Father is heard: This is my own dear Son.

Praise the Lord, you gods;
    praise his glory and power.
Praise the Lord's glorious name,
    bow down before the Holy One when he appears.

The Lord's voice is heard on the seas;
    the glorious God thunders,
    and his voice echoes over the ocean.
The Lord's voice is heard
    in all its might and majesty!

The Lord's voice breaks the cedars,
    even the cedars of Lebanon.
He causes the mountains of Lebanon to jump like
    calves,
    and Mount Hermon to leap like a young bull.

The Lord's voice makes the lightning flash.
His voice makes the desert shake;
    he shakes the desert of Kadesh.
The Lord's voice makes the deer give birth,
    and leaves the trees stripped bare,
    while in his temple all shout, "Glory to God!"

The Lord rules over the deep waters;
    he rules as king for ever.
The Lord gives strength to his people,
    and blesses them with peace.

Glory to the Father and to the Son and to the Holy
    Spirit;
  as in the beginning, so now, and for ever. Amen.

Ant. Today the heavens are opened and the voice of
    the Father is heard: This is my own dear Son.

Psalm Prayer

Let us pray (pause for silent prayer)
Father in heaven,
you revealed Christ as your Son
by the voice that spoke over the waters of the Jordan.
May all who share in the sonship of Christ
follow in his path of service,
and reflect the glory of his kingdom
even to the ends of the earth,
for he is Lord for ever and ever.
  Amen.

Reading   **Acts 10:37-39**

You know of the great event that took place throughout all of Judea, beginning in Galilee, after the baptism
that John preached. You know about Jesus of Nazareth, how God poured out on him the Holy Spirit and
power. He went everywhere, doing good and healing
all who were under the power of the Devil, for God
was with him. We are witnesses of all that he did in
the country of the Jews and in Jerusalem.

Response

Here is the Lamb of God.
  Who takes away the sin of the world.

Canticle of Mary   **See page 256**

Ant. O Savior of the world,
  out of all your creation
  you selected servants to reveal your mysteries:
  From among the angels, Gabriel;
  From the human race, the Virgin;
  From the heavens, a star;
  From the waters, the River Jordan,
  by which you washed away the sins of the world.

Let Us Pray

Lord Jesus, servant of God, in whom the Father is well
  pleased,
 Lord, have mercy on us.
Lord Jesus, whom the Father anointed with the Holy
  Spirit and with power,
 Lord, have mercy on us.
Lord Jesus, God's chosen one, upon whom the Spirit
  descends and remains,
 Lord, have mercy on us.
Lord Jesus, you baptize all who believe in you with the
  Holy Spirit and with fire,
 Lord, have mercy on us.
Lord Jesus, you are the Lamb of God who consecrates
  the world and gives us peace.
 Lord, have mercy on us.

(spontaneous prayer)

Evening Prayer

Father,
your only Son revealed himself to us by becoming man.
May we who share in his humanity,
come to share in his divinity,
for he lives and reigns with you and the Holy Spirit,
one God, for ever and ever.
 Amen.

Apostles' Creed   **Lord's Prayer**

A Christmas Devotion

I. Lord Jesus,
> you proceeded from the bosom of the eternal
> Father for our salvation,
> and were conceived by the power of the Holy
> Spirit, not disdaining the Virgin's womb.

Word made flesh, Emmanuel our God,
> **have mercy on us.**

II. Lord Jesus,
> through the visitation of your blessed Mother
> to her cousin Elizabeth,
> John the Baptist, your herald and forerunner,
> was filled with the Holy Spirit,
> and danced with joy in his mother's womb.

Word made flesh, Emmanuel our God,
> **have mercy on us.**

III. Lord Jesus,
> though God by nature,
> you did not parade your equality with God,
> but became as men are,
> and were enclosed for nine months in Mary's
> womb.

Word made flesh, Emmanuel our God,
> **have mercy on us.**

IV. Lord Jesus,
> you were born in Bethlehem of Judea, the city
> of David,
> you were wrapped in swaddling clothes and
> laid in a manger,
> you were heralded by angelic choirs
> and visited by wondering shepherds.

Word made flesh, Emmanuel our God,
> **have mercy on us.**

All glory Jesus be to you
For evermore the Virgin's Son,
To Father and to Paraclete
Be praise while endless ages run!

Christ is now near to us, alleluia.
Come, let us adore him, alleluia.

V. Lord Jesus,
   on the eighth day after your birth,
   you were circumcised according to the Law
     of Moses,
   and given the holy name of Jesus,
   the name the angel had revealed to Mary and
     Joseph before your conception.
**Word made flesh, Emmanuel our God,
   have mercy on us.**

VI. Lord Jesus,
   by the leading of a star,
   you were revealed to wise men from the East;
   they adored you on the lap of Mary
   and honored you with mystical gifts:
     gold, frankincense and myrrh.
**Word made flesh, Emmanuel our God,
   have mercy on us.**

VII. Lord Jesus,
   forty days after your birth,
   at your presentation in the Temple according
     to the Law,
   the aged Simeon received you into his arms
   and the prophetess Anna revealed you to
     Israel.
**Word made flesh, Emmanuel our God,
   have mercy on us.**

VIII. Lord Jesus,
> after the visit of the Magi,
> an angel of the Lord appeared to Joseph in
> a dream,
> and commanded him to escape into Egypt
> in the dead of night.

**Word made flesh, Emmanuel our God,
have mercy on us.**

> All glory Jesus be to you
> For evermore the Virgin's Son
> To Father and to Paraclete
> Be praise while endless ages run!

> Christ is born for us, alleluia,
> **Come, let us adore him, alleluia.**

IX. Lord Jesus,
> your flight into Egypt snatched you from a
> cruel death at Herod's hands,
> but a voice was heard in Ramah, sobbing
> and lamenting,
> Rachel weeping for her children,
> refusing to be comforted,
> because they were no more.

**Word made flesh, Emmanuel our God,
have mercy on us.**

X. Lord Jesus,
> after Herod's death,
> the angel of the Lord appeared again to
> Joseph in a dream,
> and recalled you to the land of Israel,
> where you settled in Nazareth of Galilee.

**Word made flesh, Emmanuel our God,
have mercy on us.**

XI. Lord Jesus,
> in the humble home of Nazareth,
> you lived under the authority of your parents,
> you were known as the carpenter's son,
> and you grew in wisdom and in age,
>> and in favor with God and with men.

**Word made flesh, Emmanuel our God,
have mercy on us.**

XII. Lord Jesus,
> when you were twelve years old,
> at Passover you stayed behind in Jerusalem,
> and after three days your parents found you
> in the Temple,
> sitting among the doctors, listening to them
> and asking them questions.

**Word made flesh, Emmanuel our God,
have mercy on us.**

All glory Jesus be to you
For evermore the Virgin's Son,
To Father and to Paraclete
Be praise while endless ages run!

The Word was made flesh, alleluia.
And lived among us, alleluia.

Let Us Pray:
Almighty and everlasting God, Lord of heaven
and earth,
who reveal yourself to little ones,
grant that we who recall and venerate
the mysteries of your Son's childhood,
may embrace their spirit of humility
and so come at last to the kingdom of heaven
which he promised to those who accepted it
as little children.
We ask this through the same Christ our Lord.
Amen.

111

THE SACRED TRIPOD: Prayer
Fasting
Almsgiving

THE FORTY DAYS
OF LENT

LENT—Sunday Morning

Blessed be the kingdom of God, the Father, the Son
    and the Holy Spirit.
    Now and for ever. Amen.
O Lord, open my lips.
    And my mouth shall declare your praise.

The Beatitudes   **Lk 6:20-26**

Happy are you poor:
    the Kingdom of God is yours!
Happy are you who are hungry now:
    you will be filled!
Happy are you who weep now:
    you will laugh!
Happy are you when men hate you,
    and reject you and insult you,
and say that you are evil,
    because of the Son of Man!
Be happy when that happens and dance for joy,
    for a great reward is kept for you in heaven.

But how terrible for you who are rich now:
    you have had your easy life!
How terrible for you who are full now:
    you will go hungry!
How terrible for you who laugh now:
    you will mourn and weep!
How terrible when all men speak well of you;
    for their ancestors said the very same things
    to the false prophets.

Glory to the Father and to the Son and to the Holy
    Spirit;
    as in the beginning, so now, and for ever. Amen.

Collect Prayer

Let us pray (pause for silent prayer)
Night and day both belong to you, O Lord;
may Jesus Christ, the Sun of righteousness,
continue to dwell in our hearts
and put to flight the darkness of all wrong-thinking.
Grant this through Christ our Lord.
   Amen.

Reading   Dt 6:4-9

Hear, O Israel! The LORD is our God, the LORD
alone! Therefore, you shall love the LORD your God,
with all your heart, and with all your soul, and with all
your strength. Take to heart these words which I en-
join on you today. Drill them into your children.
Speak of them at home and abroad, whether you are
busy or at rest. Bind them at your wrist as a sign and
let them be as a pendant on your forehead. Write them
on the doorposts of your houses and on your gates.

Response

You are my defender and protector!
   You are my God. In you I trust.

Canticle of Zachary   Lk 1:67-79

Ant. The Lord is our God, the Lord alone!

Blessed be the Lord, the God of Israel;
   he has come to his people and set them free.
He has raised up for us a mighty Savior,
   born of the house of his servant David.

Through his holy prophets he promised of old
    that he would save us from our enemies,
    from the hands of all who hate us.
He promised to show mercy to our fathers
    and to remember his holy covenant.

This was the oath he swore to our father Abraham,
    to set us free from our enemies' hand,
free to worship him without fear,
    holy and righteous in his sight
    all the days of our life.

You, my child, shall be called the prophet of the Most
      High,
    for you will go before the Lord to prepare his way,
to give his people knowledge of salvation
    by forgiveness of their sins.

In the tender compassion of our God
    the dawn from on high shall break upon us,
to shine on those who dwell in darkness and the
      shadow of death,
    and to guide our feet on the road to peace.

Glory to the Father and to the Son and to the Holy
      Spirit;
    as in the beginning, so now, and for ever. Amen.

Ant. The Lord is our God, the Lord alone!

Morning Prayer

God and Father of our Lord Jesus Christ,
build us up in faith and truth and in all gentleness,
without anger and in patient endurance;

number us among your saints
and count us among those who believe in Jesus
and in you, Father, who raised him from the dead.
Grant this through the same Christ,
the eternal High Priest and Son of God,
who lives and reigns with you and the Holy Spirit,
now and for ever.
   Amen.

Apostles' Creed   **Lord's Prayer**

Let us offer ourselves to God as a gift,
His most precious possession and most proper to
   himself.
Let us give back to the image what is made in that
   image.
Let us recognize the principle of our being.
Let us become like unto Christ,
Since Christ became like unto us.
Let us become gods for his sake,
Since he became man for ours.

                              St. Gregory Nazianzen

LENT—Sunday Evening

Light and peace in Jesus Christ our Lord.
Thanks be to God.

Psalm 19^b: The Law of the Lord

Ant. Your will be done, on earth as in heaven.
(Mt 6:10)

The law of the Lord is perfect;
it gives new life.
The commands of the Lord are trustworthy,
giving wisdom to those who lack it.
The rules of the Lord are right,
and those who obey them are happy.
His commandments are completely just
and give understanding to the mind.
The worship of the Lord is good;
it will continue for ever.

The judgments of the Lord are just,
they are always fair.
They are more desirable than gold,
even the finest gold.
They are sweeter than honey,
even the purest honey.
They give knowledge to me, your servant;
I am rewarded for obeying them.

No one can see his own errors;
deliver me from hidden faults!
Keep me safe, also, from open sins;
don't let them rule over me.
Then I shall be perfect
and free from terrible sin.

May my words and my thoughts be acceptable to you,
O Lord, my refuge and my redeemer!

Glory to the Father and to the Son and to the Holy
    Spirit;
    as in the beginning, so now, and for ever. Amen.

Ant. Your will be done, on earth as in heaven.

Psalm Prayer

Let us pray (pause for silent prayer)
Lord God almighty,
you are our teacher and our lawgiver.
May your commandments be as sweet as honey to us,
your will the very center of our existence,
that we may truly worship you
in union with all your saints,
now and for ever.
    Amen.

Reading   Acts 13:26-30

My brothers, descendants of Abraham, and all Gen-
tiles here who worship God: it is to us this message
of salvation has been sent! For the people who live in
Jerusalem, and their leaders, did not know that he is
the Savior, nor did they understand the words of the
prophets that are read every Sabbath day. Yet they
made the prophets' words come true by condemning
Jesus. And even though they could find no reason to
pass the death sentence on him, they asked Pilate to
have him put to death. And after they had done
everything that the Scriptures say about him, they
took him down from the cross and placed him in a
grave. But God raised him from the dead.

Response

Repent and believe in the Good News.
    The kingdom of God is at hand.

Canticle of Mary   **Lk 1:46-55**

Ant. The Lord wills not the death of the sinner
        but rather that he be converted and live. (Ez
        33:11)

My soul proclaims the greatness of the Lord,
        my spirit rejoices in God my Savior;
for he has looked with favor on his lowly servant,
        and from this day all generations will call me
        blessed.

The Almighty has done great things for me:
        holy is his Name.
He has mercy on those who fear him
        in every generation.

He has shown the strength of his arm,
        he has scattered the proud in their conceit.
He has cast down the mighty from their thrones,
        and has lifted up the lowly.
He has filled the hungry with good things,
        and sent the rich away empty-handed.

He has come to the help of his servant Israel,
        for he remembered his promise of mercy,
the promise he made to our fathers,
        to Abraham and his children for ever.

Glory to the Father and to the Son and to the Holy
        Spirit;
        as in the beginning, so now, and for ever. Amen.

Ant. The Lord wills not the death of the sinner, but
        rather that he be converted and live.

Let Us Pray

Lord Jesus Christ, grant us pardon and peace.
   Lord, have mercy.
Lord Jesus Christ, forgive our sins and neglect.
   Lord, have mercy.
Lord Jesus Christ, give us true faith and undying hope
   in your love for us.
   Lord, have mercy.
Lord Jesus Christ, unite us to the worship of the
   whole company of heaven.
   Lord, have mercy.
Lord Jesus Christ, bring us to eternal life and unfading
   light.
   Lord, have mercy.

(spontaneous prayer)

Evening Prayer

May the incense of our repentant prayer
ascend before you, O Lord,
and may your loving kindness descend upon us,
that with purified minds we may sing your praises
with the whole heavenly host
and glorify you for ever and ever.
   Amen.

Apostles' Creed   **Lord's Prayer**

Religion is adoration.
   A religion without adoration
   is like a triangle with one side left out.
                                    Friedrich von Huegel

Our Father in Heaven:

Holy be your name—
Your name is holy above all other names
and must be venerated above all other names,
and especially by me, your child of grace.
May I live and act so as to hallow your name in the
  sight of all.

Your kingdom come—
May your kingdom be my life's center,
the principal point of my desires.
Let it be to me a state of grace here and now
and a state of glory in the world to come.

Your will be done—
Let self-will depart from me.
Let your holy and gracious will be done in me and
  by me,
as it is in heaven by saints and angels.

Give us today our daily bread—
Give me what I need for health and peace.
Fix my heart on things above, not on things of earth.
Give me the bread from heaven for my salvation.

Forgive us our sins—
Forgive me my debts, the huge sum of debts,
shameful falls, frequent relapses, daily wallowings.
With God there is mercy and plenteous redemption.

As we forgive those who sin against us—
Help me to love my enemies
and pray for those who mistreat and persecute me.
Teach me to forgive as I am forgiven.

Do not bring us to the test—
Mindful of my frailty,
save me from trial and temptation
and be my Savior on the great and final day.

But deliver us from evil—
From the world, the flesh and the devil.
From the evils of the present age and of the age to
come.

From the evils of punishment which we so richly
deserve.
From all evils, past, present and future.
From all these deliver me, good Lord.

**For the kingdom, the power and the glory are yours
now and for ever.**
Bishop Lancelot Andrewes (altered)

LENT—Monday Morning

Our help is in the name of the Lord,
  The maker of heaven and earth.
O Lord, open my lips.
  And my mouth shall declare your praise.

Psalm 36ᵇ: The Goodness of God

Ant. Because of your light, O Christ, we see the light.

Lord, your constant love reaches the heavens,
  your faithfulness extends to the skies.
Your righteousness is firm like the great mountains,
  your judgments are like the depths of the sea.
You, Lord, care for men and animals.

How precious, God, is your constant love!
  Men find protection under the shadow of your
    wings.
They feast on the abundant food from your house;
  you give them to drink from the river of your
    goodness.
You are the source of all life,
  and because of your light we see the light.

Continue to love those who know you
  and to do good to those who are righteous.
Do not let proud men attack me
  or wicked men make me run away.
See where evil men have fallen!
  There they lie, unable to rise.

Glory to the Father and to the Son and to the Holy
    Spirit;
  as in the beginning, so now, and for ever. Amen.

Ant. Because of your light, O Christ, we see the light.

Psalm Prayer

Let us pray (pause for silent prayer)
Lord of life,
in your mercy hear our morning prayers,
protect us under the shadow of your cross
and make us always walk in your light,
for you are our Brother and our Savior,
O Christ our Lord,
living and reigning for ever and ever.
   Amen.

Reading   **Is 1:16-18**

Come now, let us set things right, says the Lord:
Though your sins be like scarlet, they may become
white as snow; though they be crimson red, they may
become white as wool. If you are willing and obey,
you shall eat the good things of the land; but if you
refuse and resist, the sword shall consume you: for
the mouth of the Lord has spoken!

Response

Remove my sin, O Lord, and I will be clean.
   Wash me, and I will be whiter than snow.

Canticle of Zachary   **See page 255**

Ant. Blessed be the Lord who has come to us and set
         us free.

Morning Prayer

God our Father,
each year you purify your Church
by the observance of Lent.
Help us in our annual preparation for Easter,

wash us clean from all our sins
and show us how to combine self-denial and good
   deeds.
We ask this through Christ our Lord.
   Amen.

Apostles' Creed   **Lord's Prayer**

**When men are animated by the charity of Christ,
they feel united,
   and the needs, sufferings and joys of others
   are felt as their own.**

Pope John XXIII

126

LENT—Monday Evening

Light and peace in Jesus Christ our Lord.
  Thanks be to God.

Psalm 31:1-8: A Prayer of Trust in God

Ant. Father, into your hands I commend my spirit.
  (Lk 23:46)

I come to you, Lord, for protection;
  never let me be defeated.
You are a righteous God;
  save me, I pray!
  Hear me! Save me now!
Be my refuge, to protect me;
  my defense to save me.

You are my refuge and defense;
  guide me and lead me as you have promised.
Keep me safe from the trap that has been set for me;
  you are my shelter.
  I place myself in your care.
You will save me, Lord;
  you are a faithful God.

You hate those who worship false gods;
  but I trust in you.
I will be glad and rejoice,
  because of your constant love.
You see my suffering;
  you know my trouble.
You have not let my enemies capture me;
  you have kept me safe.

Glory to the Father and to the Son and to the Holy
    Spirit;
  as in the beginning, so now, and for ever. Amen.

Ant. Father, into your hands I commend my spirit.

Psalm Prayer

Let us pray (pause for silent prayer)
Father,
on the cross Jesus placed himself entirely in your care
and surrendered himself totally to your will.
May his full trust in you
strengthen our confidence in your constant love.
We ask this through the same Christ our Lord.
   Amen.

Reading   **Rom 5:6-10**

When we were still helpless, Christ died for the wicked, at the time that God chose. It is a difficult thing for someone to die for a righteous person. It may be that someone might dare to die for a good person. But God has shown us how much he loves us: it was while we were still sinners that Christ died for us! By his death we are now put right with God; how much more, then, will we be saved by him from God's wrath. We were God's enemies, but he made us his friends through the death of his Son.

Response

Christ will cover you with the wings of his cross.
   You will be safe under his care.

Canticle of Mary   **See page 256**

Ant. My soul proclaims the greatness of the Lord,
      for he has looked with favor on his lowly servant.

Let Us Pray

For neighborly concern and fraternal affection, we
    pray.
    Lord, have mercy.
For those who await our care and practical help, we
    pray.
    Lord, have mercy.
For the heavily burdened and afflicted, we pray.
    Lord, have mercy.
For the mentally handicapped and diseased, we pray.
    Lord, have mercy.
For the friendless and abandoned, we pray.
    Lord, have mercy.

(spontaneous prayer)

Evening Prayer

Heavenly Father,
you have solemnly promised to hear the prayers
of those who address themselves to you
in the name of Jesus.
Convert our hearts and our hands to your purposes
that we may work and pray for the world's salvation.
Grant this through Christ our Lord.
    Amen.

Apostles' Creed   **Lord's Prayer**

The royal realm of Jesus is founded on a tree
    and they who hope in him shall have eternal life.
                                    Epistle of Barnabas

129

AS MY HEART OPENS UP

As my heart opens up
  under your touch
    I hear your call to death Jesus
      faint,
        whispering in peace
          offering my flesh in sacrifice
          waiting,
            waiting tenderly for my hour
            knowing that I am
          hidden
        in the hand
      the heart
      the womb
    of your father
  I await in silence
the wedding.

Jean Vanier

LENT—Tuesday Morning

Glory be to God in the Church and in Christ Jesus.
From generation to generation for ever. Amen.
O Lord, open my lips.
And my mouth shall declare your praise.

Psalm 43: Homesick for God's Altar

Ant. Send us your light and your truth, O Christ our
    Lord.

God, declare me innocent,
    and defend my cause against the ungodly;
    deliver me from lying and evil men!
You are my protector;
    why have you abandoned me?
Why must I go on suffering
    from the cruelty of my enemies?

Send your light and your truth;
    may they lead me
and bring me back to Zion, your sacred hill,
    and to your temple, where you live!
Then I will go to your altar, God,
    because you give me joy and happiness;
I will play my harp and sing praise to you,
    God, my God!

Why am I so sad?
    Why am I troubled?
I will put my hope in God,
    and once again I will praise him,
    my Savior and my God.

Glory to the Father and to the Son and to the Holy
    Spirit;
  as in the beginning, so now, and for ever. Amen.

Ant. Send us your light and your truth, O Christ our
    Lord.

Psalm Prayer

Let us pray (pause for silent prayer)
My Savior and my God,
when suffering threatens to break our spirit,
give us some ray of your light and your truth
that we may praise you once again
in union with all those who set their hope in you.
Grant this through Jesus our Lord.
  Amen.

Reading   **Is 55:6-7**

Seek the Lord while he may be found, call him while
he is near. Let the scoundrel forsake his way, and the
wicked man his thoughts; let him turn to the Lord for
mercy; to our God, who is generous in forgiving.

Response

Close your eyes to my sins, O Lord.
  And wipe out all my evil.

Canticle of Zachary   **See page 255**

Ant. The Lord has raised up a mighty Savior as he
    promised.

Morning Prayer

Heavenly Father,
guard us both from within and from without,
that we who cannot rely on our own strength
may be protected from all bodily harm
and cleansed from all evil thoughts.
We ask this through Jesus our Lord.
  Amen.

Apostles' Creed   **Lord's Prayer**

**This created world is but a small parenthesis
  in eternity.**

Sir Thomas Browne

LENT—Tuesday Evening

Light and peace in Jesus Christ our Lord.
Thanks be to God.

Psalm 32: The Joy of Being Forgiven

Ant. Happy are those who mourn: God will comfort
  them! (Mt 5:5)

Happy is the man whose sins are forgiven,
  whose transgressions are pardoned.
Happy is the man whom the Lord
    does not accuse of doing wrong,
  who is free from all deceit.

When I did not confess my sins,
  I was worn out from crying all day long.
Day and night you punished me, Lord;
  my strength was completely drained,
    as moisture is dried up by the summer heat.

Then I confessed my sins to you;
  I did not conceal my wrongdoings.
I decided to confess them to you,
  and you forgave all my transgressions.

So all your loyal people should pray to you
  in times of need;
when a great flood comes rushing,
  it will not reach them.
You are my hiding place;
  you will save me from trouble.
I sing aloud of your salvation,
  because you protect me.

The Lord says, "I will teach you
  the way you should go;
I will instruct you
  and advise you.

Don't be stupid like a horse or a mule,
    which must be controlled with a bit and bridle,
    to make it obey you."

The wicked will have to suffer,
    but those who trust in the Lord
    are protected by his constant love.
All who are righteous, be glad and rejoice,
    because of what the Lord has done!
All who obey him,
    shout for joy!

Glory to the Father and to the Son and to the Holy
      Spirit;
    as in the beginning, so now, and for ever. Amen.

Ant. Happy are those who mourn: God will comfort
    them!

Psalm Prayer

Let us pray (pause for silent prayer)
Gracious Father,
your very nature is to pardon and forgive.
Rescue us from our stupidity,
teach us to confess our sins in all honesty
and so possess the joy of being forgiven.
Grant this through Jesus our Lord.
    Amen.

Reading   **1 Cor 1:27-30**

God purposely chose what the world considers non-
sense in order to put wise men to shame, and what the
world considers weak in order to put powerful men to
shame. He chose what the world looks down on, and
despises, and thinks is nothing, in order to destroy

what the world thinks is important. This means that no single person can boast in God's presence. But God has brought you into union with Christ Jesus, and God has made Christ to be our wisdom; by him we are put right with God, we become God's own people, and are set free.

Response

The people I have formed for myself, says the Lord,
Will sing my praises.

Canticle of Mary   **See page 256**

Ant. My spirit rejoices in God my Savior;
all generations will call me blessed.

Let Us Pray

For grace, mercy and peace from on high, we pray.
Lord, have mercy.
For the destruction of all demonic powers, we pray.
Lord, have mercy.
For those who serve the needs and defend the rights of mankind, we pray.
Lord, have mercy.
For peace and good will among states and peoples, we pray.
Lord, have mercy.
For the elimination of slavery, exploitation and war, we pray.
Lord, have mercy.

(spontaneous prayer)

Evening Prayer

Almighty and everlasting God,
you want to establish justice and peace everywhere.

*Help us to discover your divine purposes
and to work for the honor and glory of your kingdom.
We ask this through Christ our Lord.*
   Amen.

Apostles' Creed   **Lord's Prayer**

**Those who hold erroneous opinions
   hold aloof from Eucharist and prayer,
   because they do not confess that the Eucharist
   is the flesh of our Savior Jesus Christ,
   which suffered for our sins,
   and which the Father in his loving-kindness
   raised from the dead.**
                              St. Ignatius of Antioch

FOR THOSE WHO HAVE FALLEN ASLEEP IN CHRIST

The Lord will open to them the gates of
    paradise,
  and they will return to that homeland
  where there is no death, but only lasting joy.

Give them eternal rest, O Lord,
  and let them share your glory.

O God, our Creator and Redeemer,
  by your power Christ conquered death
  and returned to you in glory.
  May all your people who have gone before
    us in faith
  share his victory
  and enjoy the vision of your glory for ever,
  where Christ lives and reigns with you and
    the Holy Spirit,
  one God, for ever and ever.
Amen.

Roman Missal

Blessed be the Father, the Word and the Holy Spirit.
For these three are one.
O Lord, open my lips.
And my mouth shall declare your praise.

Psalm 65: 1-8: Thanksgiving for God's Bounty

Ant. O Father, Lord of heaven and earth, I thank
you! (Mt 11:25)

God, people must praise you in Zion
and give you what they have promised,
because you answer prayers.
All men shall come to you
on account of their sins.
Our faults defeat us,
but you forgive them.
Happy are those whom you choose,
whom you bring to live in your sanctuary!
We shall be satisfied with the good things of your
house,
the blessings of your sacred temple!

You answer us, God our Savior,
and you save us by doing wonderful things.
People all over the world,
and across the distant seas, trust in you.
You set the mountains in place by your strength,
showing your mighty power.
You calm the roar of the seas
and the noise of the waves;
you calm the uproar of the peoples.
The whole world is afraid,
because of the great things that you have done.
Your actions bring shouts of joy
from one end of the earth to the other.

Glory to the Father and to the Son and to the Holy
    Spirit;
  as in the beginning, so now, and forever. Amen.

Ant. O Father, Lord of heaven and earth, I thank you!

Psalm Prayer

Let us pray (pause for silent prayer)
God our Savior,
you are wonderful in all you do.
Forgive our faults
and satisfy us with the truth and sacraments
of your sacred temple.
We ask this through Christ our Lord.
    Amen.

Reading   **Jer 17:7-8**

Blessed is the man who trusts in the Lord, whose hope
is the Lord. He is like a tree planted beside the waters,
that stretches out its roots to the stream. It fears not
the heat when it comes, its leaves stay green; in the
year of drought it shows no distress, but still bears
fruit.

Response

A faithful heart is what you want, O Lord.
    Fill my mind with your wisdom.

Canticle of Zachary   **See page 255**

Ant. Save us, O Lord, from the hands of all who hate
    us.

Morning Prayer

Almighty God,
hear the prayers of your humble people
and come to our assistance today and every day,
that we may know, love and serve you in this life
and be happy with you in the next.
We ask this through Christ our Lord.
   Amen.

Apostles' Creed   **Lord's Prayer**

Christ came to inherit a world already made,
   and yet he came to remake it totally.
                                        Charles Peguy

LENT—Wednesday Evening

Light and peace in Jesus Christ our Lord.
Thanks be to God.

Psalm 33: Praise of Divine Providence

Ant. Through the Word all things came to be.
   (Jn 1:3)

All you that are righteous,
   be glad because of what the Lord has done;
   praise him, all you that obey him!
Give thanks to the Lord with the harp,
   sing to him with stringed instruments.
Sing a new song to him,
   play the harp with skill, and sing aloud!

The words of the Lord are true,
   and all his works are dependable.
The Lord loves what is righteous and just;
   his constant love fills the earth.

The Lord created the heavens by his command,
   the sun, moon and stars by his spoken word.
He gathered all the seas into one place;
   he shuts up the ocean depths in storerooms.

Fear the Lord, all the earth!
   Fear him, all peoples of the world!
When he spoke, the world was created;
   at his command everything appeared.

The Lord frustrates the purposes of the nations;
   he keeps them from carrying out their plans.
But his plans endure forever,
   his purposes last eternally.
Happy is the nation whose God is the Lord;
   happy are the people he has chosen for his own!

Glory to the Father and to the Son and to the Holy
    Spirit;
    as in the beginning, so now, and for ever. Amen.

Ant. Through the Word all things came to be.

Psalm Prayer

Let us pray (pause for silent prayer)
Creator and Redeemer of the world,
your great plan, your eternal purpose
is to bring the whole universe back to you
through the Word made flesh, our Lord Jesus Christ.
Make us that happy people
who cooperate in the carrying out of your will for us
and who bear witness in word and in deed
to your constant love.
We ask this through the same Christ our Lord.
    Amen.

Reading   **Eph 4:30-32**

Do not make God's Holy Spirit sad; for the Spirit is
God's mark of ownership on you, a guarantee that the
Day will come when God will set you free. Get rid
of all bitterness, passion and anger. No more shouting
or insults! No more hateful feelings of any sort!
Instead, be kind and tender-hearted to one another,
and forgive one another, as God has forgiven you in
Christ.

Response

God will put his angels in charge of you.
    To protect you wherever you go.

Canticle of Mary   **See page 256**

Ant. The Almighty has done great things for me,
   holy is his Name.

Let Us Pray

Lord Jesus, grant us heartfelt repentance for all our
   sins.
   Lord, have mercy.
Lord Jesus, deliver us from a sudden and unprovided
   death.
   Lord, have mercy.
Lord Jesus, save us from disease, famine and war.
   Lord, have mercy.
Lord Jesus, guide and protect the Christian people
   everywhere.
   Lord, have mercy.
Lord Jesus, have pity on the dying and on the faithful
   departed.
   Lord, have mercy.

(spontaneous prayer)

Evening Prayer

Gracious Father,
we pray to you for your holy Catholic Church.
Fill it with your truth.
Keep it in your peace.
Where it is corrupt, reform it.
Where it is in error, correct it.
Where it is right, defend it.
Where it is in want, provide for it.
Where it is divided, reunite it;
for the sake of your Son, our Savior Jesus Christ.
   Amen.

Apostles' Creed   **Lord's Prayer**

THE SORROWFUL MYSTERIES
OF THE ROSARY

1. Hail, Mary . . . and blessed is the fruit of your womb, Jesus,
   who sweat blood for us in the Garden of Gethsemane.
2. Hail, Mary . . . and blessed is the fruit of your womb, Jesus,
   who was scourged for us at the pillar.
3. Hail, Mary . . . and blessed is the fruit of your womb, Jesus,
   who was crowned with thorns for us.
4. Hail, Mary . . . and blessed is the fruit of your womb, Jesus,
   who carried his cross for us.
5. Hail, Mary . . . and blessed is the fruit of your womb, Jesus,
   who was crucified and died for us.

Lord Jesus Christ,
at your passion, as Simeon had foretold,
a sword of sorrow pierced the soul of your gracious mother.
As we reverently recall her sorrows,
may we reap the blessed fruits of your passion.
You live and reign for ever and ever.
Amen.

LENT—Thursday Morning

Blessed be the Lord our God.
The maker of heaven and earth.
O Lord, open my lips.
And my mouth shall declare your praise.

Psalm 90: O God, Our Help in Ages Past

Ant. Dust you are and unto dust you shall return.
(Gn 3:19)

Lord, you have always been our home,
from generation to generation.
Before the hills were created,
before you brought the world into being,
you are eternally God, without beginning or end.

You tell men to return to what they were;
you change them back to soil.
A thousand years to you are like one day;
they are like yesterday, already gone,
like a short hour in the night.
You carry men away like a flood;
they last no longer than a dream.
They are like weeds that sprout in the morning,
that grow and burst into bloom,
then dry up and die in the evening.

We are destroyed by your anger;
we are terrified by your fury.
You place our sins before you,
our secret sins where you can see them.

Our lifetime is cut short by your anger;
our life comes to an end like a whisper.
Seventy years is all we have—
eighty years, if we are strong;
yet all they bring us is worry and trouble;
life is soon over, and we are gone.

Who really knows the full power of your anger?
  Who knows what fear your fury can bring?
Teach us how short our life is,
  so that we may become wise.

How long, Lord, before you relent?
  Have pity on your servants!
Fill us each morning with your constant love,
  that we may sing and be glad all our life.
Give us now as much happiness as you gave us sadness,
  during all those years when we had troubles.
Let us, your servants, see your mighty acts:
  let our descendants see your glorious might.
Lord our God, may your blessings be with us,
  and give us success in all we do!
  Yes, give us success in all we do!

Glory to the Father and to the Son and to the Holy
    Spirit;
  as in the beginning, so now, and for ever. Amen.

Ant. Dust you are and unto dust you shall return.

Psalm Prayer

Let us pray (pause for silent prayer)
Eternal God,
you alone are stable and trustworthy
in this fleeting world.
As each new day begins,
fill us with your constant love,
grant us true wisdom of heart
and help us pass this brief life in serving you.
We ask this through Jesus Christ our Lord.
  Amen.

Reading   **Ez 36:25-28**

I will sprinkle clean water upon you to cleanse you
from all your impurities, and from all your idols I will
cleanse you. I will give you a new heart and place a
new spirit within you, taking from your bodies your
stony hearts and giving you natural hearts. I will put
my Spirit within you and make you live. . . . You
shall be my people and I shall be your God.

Response

Create a pure heart in me, O God.
   And put a new and loyal spirit in me.

Canticle of Zachary   **See page 255**

Ant. Serve the Lord in holiness all the days of your
   life.

Morning Prayer

Merciful Father,
you are our first beginning and our last end.
Guide and guard our restless and unquiet hearts,
inspire us to love you with devotion
and to serve our fellow Christians with generosity.
We ask this through Christ our Lord.
   Amen.

Apostles' Creed   **Lord's Prayer**

When sin no longer exists we shall all be Christ's
   image,
   all shining with one and the same beauty.
                                        St. Gregory of Nyssa

LENT—Thursday Evening

Light and peace in Jesus Christ our Lord.
Thanks be to God.

Psalm 41: Prayer in Sickness and Betrayal

Ant. One of you will betray me—one who is eating
with me. (Mk 14:18)

Happy is the man who is concerned for the poor;
  the Lord will help him when he is in trouble.
The Lord will protect him and preserve his life;
  he will make him happy in the land;
  he will not abandon him to the power of his enemies.
The Lord will help him when he is sick
  and restore him to health.

I said, "I have sinned against you, Lord;
  be merciful to me and cure me!"
My enemies say bad things about me.
  They say, "When will he die and be forgotten?"
Those who come to see me are not sincere;
  they gather all the bad news about me,
  and then go out and tell it everywhere.

All who hate me whisper to each other about me,
  they imagine the worst about me.
They say, "He is fatally ill
  and will never leave his bed again."
Even my best friend, the one I trusted most,
  the one who shared my food,
  has turned against me.

Be merciful to me, Lord, and restore my health;
  and I will pay my enemies back!
I will know that you are pleased with me,
  because they will not triumph over me.
You will help me, because I do what is right;
  you will keep me in your presence forever.

Glory to the Father and to the Son and to the Holy
   Spirit;
   as in the beginning, so now, and for ever. Amen.

Ant. One of you will betray me—one who is eating
   with me.

Psalm Prayer

Let us pray (pause for silent prayer)
Lord Jesus Christ,
you experienced fully the weakness of our humanity
and were even betrayed by your friends.
By your blessed passion
be our comfort and protection
and strengthen us in our weakness.
You live and reign for ever.
   Amen.

Reading   Heb 13:12-15

Jesus died outside the city gate, in order to cleanse the
people from sin with his own blood. Let us, then, go
to him outside the camp and share his shame. For
there is no permanent city for us here on earth; we
are looking for the city which is to come. Let us, then,
always offer praise to God as our sacrifice through
Jesus; that is, let us always give thanks to his name
with our voices.

Response

Come near to God.
   And he will come near to you.

Canticle of Mary   See page 256

Ant. God has mercy on those who fear him in every
   generation.

Let Us Pray

From all evil, temptation and sin,
  Good Lord, deliver us.
From stubbornness, obstinacy and pride,
  Good Lord, deliver us.
From hard-heartedness in the face of human need,
  Good Lord, deliver us.
From dishonesty, hypocrisy and all lying,
  Good Lord, deliver us.
From the snares of the enemy and from everlasting
  death,
  Good Lord, deliver us.

(spontaneous prayer)

Evening Prayer

Grant us, O Lord,
in all our ways of life your help,
in all our perplexities your counsel,
in all our temptations your protection,
in all our sorrows your peace.
We ask through Jesus Christ our Lord.
  Amen.

Apostles' Creed   **Lord's Prayer**

The life of Jesus Christ is not in us
  unless we are ready of our own accord
  to die in order to share his passion.
                                   St. Ignatius of Antioch

FOR THE FORGIVENESS OF SINS

Lord Jesus Christ, whose will all things obey:
Pardon what I have done,
and grant that I, a sinner, may sin no more.
Lord, I believe that though I do not deserve it,
you can cleanse me from all my sins.
Lord, I know that man looks upon the face,
but you see the heart.
Send your Spirit into my innermost being,
to take possession of my soul and body.
Without you I cannot be saved.
With you to protect me I long for your
    salvation.
And now I ask you for wisdom.
Of your great goodness help and defend me.
Guide my heart, Almighty God,
that I might remember your presence
both by day and by night.
Amen.

From an ancient manuscript

LENT—Friday Morning

We adore you, O Christ, and we bless you.
For by your holy cross you have redeemed the world.
O Lord, open my lips.
And my mouth shall declare your praise.

Psalm 51: A Prayer for Forgiveness

Ant. O God, have pity on me, a sinner! (Lk 18:13)

Be merciful to me, God,
    because of your constant love;
wipe away my sins,
    because of your great mercy!
Wash away my evil,
    and make me clean from my sin!

I recognize my faults;
    I am always conscious of my sins.
I have sinned against you—only against you,
    and done what you consider evil.
So you are right in judging me;
    you are justified in condemning me.
I have been evil from the time I was born;
    from the day of my birth I have been sinful.

A faithful heart is what you want;
    fill my mind with your wisdom.
Remove my sin, and I will be clean;
    wash me, and I will be whiter than snow.
Let me hear the sounds of joy and gladness;
    and though you have crushed and broken me,
    I will be happy once again.
Close your eyes to my sins,
    and wipe out all my evil.

Create a pure heart in me, God,
    and put a new and loyal spirit in me.

Do not banish me from your presence;
   do not take your Holy Spirit away from me.
Give me again the joy that comes from your salvation,
   and make my spirit obedient.
Then I will teach sinners your commands,
   and they will turn back to you.
Spare my life, God my Savior,
   and I will gladly proclaim your righteousness.
Help me to speak, Lord,
   and I will praise you.

You do not want sacrifices,
   or I would offer them;
   you are not pleased with burnt offerings.
My sacrifice is a submissive spirit, God;
   a submissive and obedient heart you will not reject.

Glory to the Father and to the Son and to the Holy
      Spirit;
   as in the beginning, so now, and for ever. Amen.

Ant. O God, have pity on me, a sinner!

Psalm Prayer

Let us pray (pause for silent prayer)
Almighty and merciful Father,
you freely forgive those who acknowledge their sins,
as did David the prophet-king of Israel.
Create pure hearts in us, O God,
and wash away all our sins in the precious blood
of your dear Son, our Savior Jesus Christ,
who lives and reigns with you and the Holy Spirit,
one God, for ever and ever.
   Amen.

Reading   **Is 53:2-4**

God's servant grew up like a sapling before him, like
a shoot from the parched earth; there was in him no
stately bearing to make us look at him, nor appearance
that would attract us to him. He was spurned and
avoided by men, a man of suffering accustomed to
infirmity, one of those from whom men hide their
faces, spurned, and we held him in no esteem. Yet it
was our infirmities that he bore, our sufferings that he
endured, while we thought of him as stricken, as one
smitten by God and afflicted.

Response

All you who pass by, look and see:
Is there any sorrow like the sorrow that afflicts me?

Canticle of Zachary   **See page 255**

Ant. In the tender compassion of our God the Dawn
has broken upon us.

Ant. for Good Friday: Pilate wrote a notice and put
it on the cross: "Jesus of Nazareth, the King of
the Jews." (Jn 19:20)

Morning Prayer

Almighty and everlasting God,
you willed that our Savior should become man
and undergo the torment of the cross
as an example of humility for all mankind.
Grant that we may so follow in his suffering footsteps
as to share in his glorious resurrection.
We ask this through the same Christ our Lord.
   Amen.

Apostles' Creed   **Lord's Prayer**

LENT—Friday Evening

Light and peace in Jesus Christ our Lord.
Thanks be to God.

Psalm 22:1-21 The Sufferings of the Messiah

Ant. They will mock him and scourge him and spit on
him and put him to death. (Mk 10:34)

My God, my God, why have you abandoned me?
I have cried desperately for help,
but it still does not come!
During the day I call to you, my God,
but you do not answer;
I call at night,
but get no rest.
But you are enthroned as the Holy One,
the One whom Israel praises.

Our ancestors put their trust in you;
they trusted you, and you saved them.
They called to you and escaped from danger;
they trusted in you and were not disappointed.

But I am no longer a man; I am a worm,
despised and scorned by all!
All who see me make fun of me;
they stick out their tongues and shake their heads.
"You relied on the Lord," they say. "Why doesn't he
save you?
If the Lord likes you, why doesn't he help you?"

It was you who brought me safely through birth,
and when I was a baby you kept me safe.
I have relied on you ever since I was born;
since my birth you have been my God.
Do not stay away from me!
Trouble is near,
and there is no one to help.

Many enemies surround me like bulls;
    they are all around me,
    like fierce bulls from the land of Bashan.
They open their mouths like lions,
    roaring and tearing at me.

My strength is gone,
    gone like water spilled on the ground.
All my bones are out of joint;
    my heart feels like melted wax inside me.
My throat is as dry as dust,
    and my tongue sticks to the roof of my mouth.
    You have left me for dead in the dust.

A gang of evil men is around me;
    like a pack of dogs, they close in on me;
    they tear my hands and feet.
All my bones can be seen.
    My enemies look at me and stare.
They divide my clothes among themselves
    and gamble for my robe.

Don't stay away from me, Lord!
    Hurry and help me, my Savior!
Save me from the sword;
    save my life from those dogs.
Rescue me from those lions;
    I am helpless before those wild bulls.

Glory to the Father and to the Son and to the Holy
    Spirit;
    as in the beginning, so now, and for ever. **Amen.**

Ant. They will mock him and scourge him and spit
    on him and put him to death.

Psalm Prayer

Let us pray (pause for silent prayer)
Lord Jesus Christ, suffering servant of God,
for our sake
you were unjustly condemned to death,
mocked, scourged and crowned with thorns,
pierced with nails and scorned by unbelievers.
By your holy and glorious wounds
guard us and keep us from all evil
and bring us to the victory you have won for us.
You live and reign for ever and ever.
   Amen.

Reading   1 Pt 2:21-24

Christ himself suffered for you and left you an example, so that you would follow in his steps. He com-
mitted no sin; no one ever heard a lie come from his
lips. When he was cursed he did not answer back with
a curse; when he suffered he did not threaten, but
placed his hopes in God, the righteous Judge. Christ
himself carried our sins on his body to the cross, so
that we might die to sin and live for righteousness.

Response

Christ walked the path of obedience to death.
   His death on the cross.

Canticle of Mary   See page 256

Ant. The Lord casts down the mighty from their
   thrones and lifts up the lowly.

Ant. for Good Friday: Jesus said, "It is finished!"
   Then he bowed his head and died. (Jn 19:30)

158

Let Us Pray

Christ, our true God, of your own free will, you accepted the dread passion for us and for our salvation.
   Lord, have mercy.
Friend of mankind, you embraced the terrible cross and the burial in the tomb.
   Lord, have mercy.
You were seen without beauty to give back to all the splendor of God.
   Lord, have mercy.
Like a seed you were buried in the ground and sprang up a hundredfold.
   Lord, have mercy.
Through your divine death we are all delivered from death and decay.
   Lord, have mercy.
Your cross vanquished hell and put dark death to flight.
   Lord, have mercy.
Through your love and compassion you have saved all the nations of the earth.
   Lord, have mercy.

(spontaneous prayer)

Evening Prayer

Lord Jesus Christ, Son of the living God,
at day's end you rested in the tomb
and made the grave a bed of hope for those who
   believe in you.

Life of the world,
when our bodies lie in the dust of death,
may our souls live with you
for ever and ever.
   Amen.

Apostles' Creed   **Lord's Prayer**

Fasting is only one branch of a large and momentous
   duty,
   the subdual of ourselves to Christ.
   We must surrender to him all we have, all we are.
   We must keep nothing back.

John Henry Newman

THE BLESSED PASSION

Blessed art thou, O Lord,
for the holy sufferings of this day.
By thy saving sufferings on this day
  save us, O Lord.
    By the sweat bloody, in clots,
      the soul in agony,
      the head wreathed with thorns driven
        in with the rods,
      the eyes filled with tears,
      the ears full of opprobries,
      the mouth given to drink of vinegar
        and gall,
      the face shamefully befouled with
        spitting,
      the neck loaded with the burden of the
        cross,
      the back ploughed with the weals and
        gashes of whips,
      the hands and feet digged through,
      the strong crying "eli, eli,"
      the heart pierced with a spear,
      the water and blood forth flowing,
        the body broken,
        the blood outpoured.

                    Bishop Lancelot Andrewes

LENT—Saturday Morning

Our help is in the name of the Lord.
The maker of heaven and earth.
O Lord, open my lips.
And my mouth shall declare your praise.

Psalm 92: Praise of God's Providence

Ant. Happy are those whose greatest desire is to do
what God requires. (Mt 3:6)

How good it is to give thanks to the Lord,
to sing in your honor, Most High God,
to proclaim your constant love every morning,
and your faithfulness every night,
with the music of stringed instruments,
and with melody on the harp.
Your mighty acts, Lord, make me glad;
because of what you have done I sing for joy.

How great are your acts, Lord!
How deep are your thoughts!
Here is something a fool cannot know,
a stupid man cannot understand:
the wicked may grow like weeds,
and all evildoers may prosper;
yet they will be totally destroyed,
because you, Lord, are supreme for ever.

The righteous will flourish like palm trees;
they will grow like the cedars of Lebanon.
They are like trees planted in the house of the Lord,
that flourish in the temple of our God,
that still bear fruit in old age,
and are always green and strong.
This shows that the Lord is just;
in him, my defender, there is no wrong.

Glory to the Father and to the Son and to the Holy
    Spirit;
  as in the beginning, so now, and for ever. Amen.

Ant. Happy are those whose greatest desire is to do
    what God requires.

Psalm Prayer

Let us pray (pause for silent prayer)
Most High God, rock of our salvation,
we give you thanks for the coming of a new day
in which we can celebrate your mighty deeds on our
    behalf.
Plant us deep in your designs
and make us bear fruit for eternity.
We ask this through Christ our Lord.
    Amen.

Reading   **Mal 1:11**

From the rising of the sun, even to its setting, my name
is great among the nations; and everywhere they bring
sacrifice to my name, and a pure offering; for great is
my name among the nations, says the Lord of hosts.

Response

My sacrifice is a submissive spirit, O God.
    A submissive and obedient heart you will not reject.

Canticle of Zachary   **See page 255**

Ant. Shine on those who dwell in darkness, O Lord,
    and guide our feet on the road to peace.

Ant. for Holy Saturday: I have authority over death
    and the world of the dead, says the Lord Jesus.
    (Rv 1:18)

Morning Prayer

Father,
look mercifully on those for whom Christ freely died,
so that by your grace and protection
we may serve you faithfully in your holy Church
to the honor and glory of your name.
Grant this through Jesus our Lord.
   Amen.

Apostles' Creed   **Lord's Prayer**

Good Friday must give way to the triumphant music of Easter.

Martin Luther King

LENT—Saturday Evening

Light and peace in Jesus Christ our Lord.
Thanks be to God.

Psalm 57: A Confident Prayer for Help

Ant. God, show your greatness in the sky,
and your glory over all the earth!

Be merciful to me, God, be merciful,
because I come to you for safety.
In the shadow of your wings I find protection,
until all danger is past.
I call to God, the Most High,
to God, who supplies all my needs.
He will answer from heaven and save me;
he will defeat my attackers.
God will show me his constant love and faithfulness.

I lie down among lions,
who are ready to devour men.
Their teeth are like spears and arrows;
their tongues are like sharp swords.

Ant. God, show your greatness in the sky,
and your glory over all the earth!

My enemies have spread a net to catch me;
I am overcome with distress.
They dug a pit in my path,
but fell into it themselves.

I am ready, God;
I am completely ready!
I will sing and praise you!
Wake up, my soul!
Wake up, my harp and lyre!
I will wake up the sun!

I will thank you among the nations, Lord!
    I will praise you among the peoples!
Your constant love reaches up to heaven,
    your faithfulness to the skies.

Ant. God, show your greatness in the sky,
    and your glory over all the earth!

Glory to the Father and to the Son and to the Holy
    Spirit;
    as in the beginning, so now, and for ever. Amen.

Ant. God, show your greatness in the sky,
    and your glory over all the earth!

Psalm Prayer

Let us pray (pause for silent prayer)
Lord Jesus Christ,
when we are overwhelmed by trials and temptations,
may we find protection in the shadow of your cross,
while we await in sure and certain hope
the full revelation of your victory over death and hell.
You live and reign for ever and ever.
    Amen.

Reading   **1 Pt 1:18-21**

You know what was paid to set you free from the
worthless manner of life you received from your ancestors. It was not something that loses its value, such
as silver or gold; you were set free by the costly sacrifice of Christ, who was like a lamb without defect or
spot. He had been chosen by God before the founda-
tion of the world, and was revealed in these last days
for your sake. Through him you believe in God, who
raised him from death and gave him glory; and so your
faith and hope are fixed on God.

Response

Conquering Lion, of the tribe of Judah,
  Rouse up your kingly might and save us.

Canticle of Mary   **See page 256**

Ant. The Lord remembers his promise of mercy.

Ant. for Holy Saturday: They made the grave secure
  by putting a seal on the stone and leaving the
  guard on watch. (Mt 27:66)

Let Us Pray

For the Church universal and here at hand, we pray.
  Lord, have mercy.
For ministers of the gospel who speak the truth in love,
  we pray.
  Lord, have mercy.
For the reconciliation of our differences, we pray.
  Lord, have mercy.
For the full employment of our gifts and talents, we
  pray.
  Lord, have mercy.
For our beloved dead who have fallen asleep in Christ,
  we pray.
  Lord, have mercy.

(spontaneous prayer)

Evening Prayer

Lord Jesus Christ,
you loved us and delivered yourself up for us
as an agreeable and fragrant sacrifice to God;
rescue us from our former darkness

*and teach us to walk as children of the light
in all goodness, justice and truth.
You live and reign for ever and ever.*
   Amen.

Apostles' Creed

                                              Lord's Prayer

**Observe those who hold erroneous opinions
   concerning the grace of Jesus Christ
   which has come to us
   and see how they run counter to the mind of God!
They concern themselves with neither
   works of charity,
   nor widows, nor orphans, nor the distressed,
   nor those in prison or out of it,
   nor the hungry or thirsty.**

                                    St. Ignatius of Antioch

INVOCATION OF THE HOLY SPIRIT

Come, Holy Spirit, fill the hearts of your
      faithful
   and kindle in them the fire of your divine
   love.

When you send forth your Spirit, they are
      created,
   And you renew the face of the earth.

O God,
on the first Pentecost you instructed the hearts
      of those who believed in you
by the light of the Holy Spirit.
Under the inspiration of the same Spirit,
give us a taste for what is right and true,
and a continuing sense of his joy-bringing
      presence and power,
through Jesus Christ our Lord.
Amen.

**During the fifty days of Easter
let no one fast or kneel,
for these are days of rest and joy.**

The Testament of the Lord

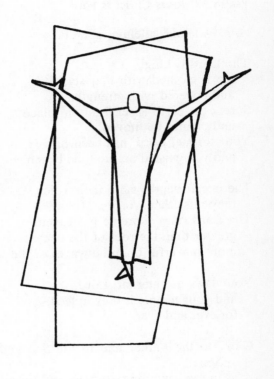

THE FIFTY DAYS
OF EASTER

EASTER—Sunday Morning

Christ is risen, alleluia.
He is risen indeed, alleluia.
O Lord, open my lips.
And my mouth shall declare your praise.

Psalm 93: Jesus Christ Is Lord

Ant. Alleluia, alleluia, alleluia!

The Lord is king!
   He is clothed with majesty,
   and covered with strength.
Surely the earth is set firmly in place
   and cannot be moved.
Your throne, Lord, has been firm from the beginning,
   and you existed before time began.

The ocean depths raise their voice, Lord;
   they raise their voice and roar.
The Lord rules supreme in heaven,
   greater than the roar of the ocean,
   more powerful than the waves of the sea.

Your laws are eternal, Lord,
   and your temple is holy indeed,
   for ever and ever.

Glory to the Father and to the Son and to the Holy
   Spirit;
   as in the beginning, so now, and for ever. Amen.

Ant. Alleluia, alleluia, alleluia!

Psalm Prayer

Let us pray (pause for silent prayer)
Lord Jesus Christ,
by virtue of your rising from the dead,
you are clothed in majesty
and covered with divine strength.
Be the supreme ruler of our hearts and minds,
free us for your service
and establish us firmly on the rock of faith.
You live and reign for ever and ever.
  Amen.

Reading   Mk 16:1-7

After the Sabbath was over, Mary Magdalene, Mary the mother of James, and Salome bought spices to go and anoint the body of Jesus. Very early on Sunday morning, at sunrise, they went to the grave. On the way they said to one another, "Who will roll away the stone from the entrance to the grave for us?" (It was a very large stone.) Then they looked up and saw that the stone had already been rolled back. So they entered the grave, where they saw a young man, sitting at the right, who wore a white robe—and they were filled with alarm. "Don't be alarmed," he said. "You are looking for Jesus of Nazareth, who was nailed to the cross. But he is not here—he has risen!"

Response

We adore your cross, O Lord, alleluia.
  And we praise and glorify your holy resurrection, alleluia.

Te Deum

You are God: we praise you;
  You are the Lord: we acclaim you;
You are the eternal Father:
  All creation worships you.

To you all angels, all the powers of heaven,
  Cherubim and Seraphim, sing in endless praise:
Holy, holy, holy Lord, God of power and might,
  heaven and earth are full of your glory.

The glorious company of apostles praise you.
  The noble fellowship of prophets praise you.
  The white-robed army of martyrs praise you.

Throughout the world the holy Church acclaims you:
  Father, of majesty unbounded,
  your true and only Son, worthy of all worship,
  and the Holy Spirit, advocate and guide.

You, Christ, are the king of glory,
  eternal Son of the Father.
When you became man to set us free
  you did not disdain the Virgin's womb.

You overcame the sting of death
  and opened the kingdom of heaven to all believers.
You are seated at God's right hand in glory.
  We believe that you will come and be our judge.

Come, then, Lord, sustain your people,
  bought with the price of your own blood,
and bring us with your saints
  to everlasting glory.

Morning Prayer

Hear us, O God our Father,
through the new Adam, our Lord Jesus Christ,
that buried with him in baptism
and raised again by his life,
we may enjoy the indwelling of the Holy Spirit
and be absolved of all our sins.
We ask this through the same Christ our Lord.
   Amen.

Apostles' Creed   **Lord's Prayer**

We are Easter people and alleluia is our song.
                          St. Augustine of Hippo

175

EASTER—Sunday Evening

Christ is risen from the dead!
**He trampled down death by his death
and brought life to those in the grave.**

Psalm 114: A Passover Song

Ant. When we were baptized into union with Christ
Jesus, we were baptized into union with his
death. (Rom 6:3)

When the people of Israel left Egypt,
    when Jacob's descendants left that foreign land,
Judah became the Lord's holy people,
    Israel became his own possession.

The Sea of Reeds looked and ran away,
    the Jordan River stopped flowing.
The mountains skipped like goats,
    the hills skipped around like sheep.

What happened, Sea, to make you run away?
    And you, Jordan, why did you stop flowing?
Mountains, why did you skip like goats?
    Hills, why did you skip around like sheep?

Tremble, earth, at the Lord's coming,
    at the presence of the God of Jacob,
who changes rocks into pools of water,
    and stone cliffs into flowing springs.

Glory to the Father and to the Son and to the Holy
        Spirit;
    as in the beginning, so now, and for ever. Amen.

Ant. When we were baptized into union with Christ
Jesus, we were baptized into union with his
death.

Psalm Prayer

Let us pray (pause for silent prayer)
Rescuing God,
as of old you brought forth your chosen people
from the slavery of Egypt
and conducted them to a land flowing with milk and
    honey,
so now deliver the people of your new and eternal
    covenant
from the slavery of sin
and make your Church a land of spiritual plenty
and of hope for the human race.
We ask this through Jesus Christ, our risen Lord.
  Amen.

Reading   **Col 3:1-4**

You have been raised to life with Christ. Set your
hearts, then, on the things that are in heaven, where
Christ sits on his throne at the right side of God. Keep
your minds fixed on things there, not on things here on
earth. For you have died, and your life is hidden with
Christ in God. Your real life is Christ, and when he
appears, then you too will appear with him and share
his glory!

Response

Christ has been raised from death, alleluia.
  And will never die again, alleluia.

Canticle of Mary   **See page 256**

Ant. Late that Sunday evening,
        Jesus came and stood among them and said:
        Peace be with you, alleluia. (Jn 20:19)

Let Us Pray

Lord Jesus, who died for our sins and rose for our
     salvation,
  Hear us, risen Lord.
Lord Jesus, who trampled down death by your death,
  Hear us, risen Lord.
Lord Jesus, who brought life to those in the grave,
  Hear us, risen Lord.
Lord Jesus, who overcame death's sting and gave fresh
     life to our fallen world,
  Hear us, risen Lord.
Lord Jesus, our life and our resurrection,
  Hear us, risen Lord.

(spontaneous prayer)

Evening Prayer

Heavenly Father,
when Christ our Paschal Lamb was sacrificed,
he overcame death by his own dying
and restored us to life by his own rising;
in virtue of his life-giving Passover,
pour your Holy Spirit into our hearts,
fill us with awe and reverence for you
and with love and compassion for our neighbor.
We ask this through the same Christ our Lord.
  Amen.

Apostles' Creed   **Lord's Prayer**

Haste is the death of devotion.
                              St. Francis de Sales

EASTER

O Day of Resurrection!
Let us beam with festive joy!
Today indeed is the Lord's own Passover,
For from death to life, from earth to heaven
Christ has led us
As we shout the victory hymn!
   Christ has risen from the dead!

Let our hearts be spotless
As we gaze upon our dazzling Christ:
See his rising—a brilliant flash of light divine!
Let us listen,
Clearly hear him greeting us:
As we shout the victory hymn!
   Christ has risen from the dead!

Let all heaven burst with joy!
Let all the earth resound with gladness!
Let all creation dance in celebration!
For Christ has risen:
Christ, our lasting joy!
   Christ has risen from the dead!

St. John of Damascus

EASTER—Monday Morning

Christ is risen, alleluia.
He is risen indeed, alleluia.
O Lord, open my lips.
And my mouth shall declare your praise.

Psalm 27ᵃ: The Risen Lord Is Our Light and Our Salvation

Ant. I am the light of the world, says the Lord,
    alleluia. (Jn 8:12)

The Lord is my light and my salvation;
    I will fear no one.
The Lord protects me from all danger;
    I will not be afraid.

When evil men attack me and try to kill me,
    they stumble and fall.
Even if a whole army surrounds me,
    I will not be afraid;
even if my enemies attack me,
    I will still trust God.

I have asked the Lord for one thing;
    one thing only do I want:
to live in the Lord's house all my life,
    to marvel at his goodness,
    and to ask his guidance there.

In times of trouble he will protect me in his shelter;
    he will keep me safe in his temple,
    and place me securely on a high rock.
So I will triumph over my enemies around me.
    With shouts of joy I will offer sacrifices in his temple;
    I will sing, I will praise the Lord!

Glory to the Father and to the Son and to the Holy
    Spirit;
  as in the beginning, so now, and for ever. Amen.

Ant. I am the light of the world, says the Lord,
    alleluia.

Psalm Prayer

Let us pray (pause for silent prayer)
Lord Jesus Christ, true Sun and everlasting Day,
shine on the darkness of our minds,
enlighten us with the radiance of your gospel truth,
and take us to live with you in your own house
for ever and ever.
  Amen.

Reading   Acts 2:22-24

Listen to these words, men of Israel! Jesus of Nazareth
was a man whose divine mission was clearly shown to
you by the miracles, wonders, and signs which God
did through him; you yourselves know this, for it took
place here among you. God, in his own will and
knowledge, had already decided that Jesus would be
handed over to you; and you killed him, by letting
sinful men nail him to the cross. But God raised him
from the dead; he set him free from the pains of death,
for it was impossible that death should hold him
prisoner.

Response

Christ died for our sins and was buried, alleluia.
  And was raised to life on the third day, alleluia.

Canticle of Zachary   **See page 255**

Ant. I know you are looking for Jesus,
        who was nailed to the cross.
        He is not here; he has risen, alleluia. (Mt 28:5)

Morning Prayer

Lord Jesus Christ,
you have snapped the bonds of death
and ascended a conqueror from the grave.
Put away our offenses,
restore innocence to the guilty
and joy to the disheartened,
and bring us out of the prison-house of death
into the paradise for ever green,
where you live and reign for ever and ever.
    Amen.

Apostles' Creed   **Lord's Prayer**

A man can't be always defending the truth,
    there must be a time to feed on it.

                                              C. S. Lewis

EASTER—Monday Evening

Christ is risen from the dead!
**He trampled down death by his death
and brought life to those in the grave.**

Psalm 66: Praise the Living Christ

Ant. By your death, O Christ, you bought men for
God, alleluia. (Rv 5:9)

Praise God with shouts of joy, all people!
Sing to the glory of his name;
offer him glorious praise!
Say to God, "How wonderful are the things you do!
Your power is so great
that your enemies bow in fear before you.
Everyone on earth worships you;
they sing praises to you,
they sing praises to your name."

Come and see what God has done,
his wonderful acts among men.
He changed the sea into dry land;
our ancestors crossed the river on foot.
There we rejoiced
because of what he had done.
He rules forever by his might
and keeps his eyes on the nations.
Let no rebels rise against him!

Praise our God, all nations;
let your praise be heard.
He has kept us alive
and has not allowed us to fall.
You have put us to the test, God;
as silver is purified by fire,
so you have tested us.
You let us fall into a trap
and placed heavy burdens on our backs.

You let our enemies trample us;
  we went through fire and flood,
  but now you have brought us to a place of safety.

I will bring burnt offerings to your house;
  I will offer you what I promised.
I will give you what I said I would,
  when I was in trouble.
I will offer sheep to be burned on the altar;
  there will be the aroma of burning goats;
  I will sacrifice bulls and goats.

Come and listen, all who honor God,
  and I will tell you what he has done for me.
I cried to him for help;
  I was ready to praise him with songs.
If I had ignored my sins,
  the Lord would not have listened to me.
But God has indeed heard me;
  he has listened to my prayer.
I praise God,
  because he did not reject my prayer,
  or keep back his constant love from me.

Glory to the Father and to the Son and to the Holy
    Spirit;
  as in the beginning, so now, and for ever. Amen.

Ant. By your death, O Christ, you bought men for
    God, alleluia.

Psalm Prayer

Let us pray (pause for silent prayer)
God of glory,
by the preaching of the gospel
make your wonderful acts known to the whole world,

*so that all nations may sing to the praise of your name,
worshiping the Father, the Son and the Holy Spirit,
now and for ever.*
Amen.

Reading   1 Pt 1:3-5

Let us give thanks to the God and Father of our Lord
Jesus Christ! Because of his great mercy, he gave us
new life by raising Jesus Christ from the dead. This
fills us with a living hope, and so we look forward to
possess the rich blessings that God keeps for his people.
He keeps them for you in heaven, where they cannot
decay or spoil or fade away. They are for you, who
through faith are kept safe by God's power, as you
wait for the salvation which is ready to be revealed at
the end of time.

Response

When we were baptized into union with Christ Jesus,
    alleluia,
  We were baptized into union with his death, alleluia.

Canticle of Mary   See page 256

Ant. Jesus breathed on his disciples and said:
      Receive the Holy Spirit.
      If you forgive men's sins then they are forgiven,
      alleluia. (Jn 20:22-23)

Let Us Pray

Lord Jesus, our life and our resurrection,
  Hear us, risen Lord.
Lord Jesus, who established the new and eternal
    covenant in your precious blood,
  Hear us, risen Lord.

185

Lord Jesus, who set us free from the law of sin and
     death,
  Hear us, risen Lord.
Lord Jesus, pleading for us at God's right hand,
  Hear us, risen Lord.
Lord Jesus, hope of the faithful departed,
  Hear us, risen Lord.

(spontaneous prayer)

Evening Prayer

God our Father,
for our redemption you delivered up your only Son
to the death of the cross,
and by his glorious resurrection
rescued us from the power of the enemy.
Help us to die daily to sin
that we may always live with him
in the power and the glory of his risen life.
We ask this through the same Christ our Lord.
  Amen.

Apostles' Creed   **Lord's Prayer**

**Nothing will repay one so much as the constant study
and meditation of the Sacred Scriptures.**
                                        Paul Claudel

A MARIAN ANTHEM FOR EASTERTIDE

Rejoice, O Queen of Heaven, alleluia,
   The Son whom you were worthy to bear,
      alleluia,
   has arisen as he promised, alleluia.
   Pray for us to the Father, alleluia.

Rejoice and be glad, O Virgin Mary, alleluia,
   for the Lord has really risen, alleluia.

O God,
   by the resurrection of your Son, our Lord
      Jesus Christ,
   You gave joy to the world.
   Grant that through his mother, the Virgin
      Mary,
   we may obtain the joys of everlasting life.
   We ask this through the same Christ our
      Lord.
   Amen.

EASTER—Tuesday Morning

Christ is risen, alleluia.
He is risen indeed, alleluia.
O Lord, open my lips.
And my mouth shall declare your praise.

Psalm 96: Praise Our Risen Lord!

Ant. The Lord reigns from the tree, alleluia.

Sing a new song to the Lord!
Sing to the Lord, all the world!
Sing to the Lord and praise him!
Every day tell the good news that he has saved us!
Proclaim his glory to the nations,
his mighty acts to all peoples.

The Lord is great, and must be highly praised;
he must be feared more than all the gods.
The gods of all other nations are only idols,
but the Lord made the heavens.
Glory and majesty are around him,
greatness and beauty are in his temple.

All people on earth, praise the Lord!
Praise his glory and might!
Praise the Lord's glorious name;
bring an offering and come into his temple.
Bow down before the Holy One when he appears;
tremble before him, all the earth!

Say to all the nations, "The Lord is king!
The earth is set firmly in place and cannot be
moved;
he will judge all peoples with justice."
Be glad, earth and sky!
Roar, sea, and all the creatures in you;
be glad, fields, and everything in you!

Then the trees in the woods will shout for joy before
    the Lord,
  because he comes to rule the earth.
He will rule all peoples of the world
  with justice and fairness.

Glory to the Father and to the Son and to the Holy
        Spirit;
  as in the beginning, so now, and for ever. Amen.

Ant. The Lord reigns from the tree, alleluia.

Psalm Prayer

Let us pray (pause for silent prayer)
Lord Jesus Christ, victorious king,
whose triumph over death and hell
is the new song sung by all the world,
extend your gentle rule over all nations
and prepare them for your awesome coming
in glory and might.
You live and reign for ever and ever.
  Amen.

Reading   Acts 2:32-36

God has raised this very Jesus from the dead, and we
are all witnesses to this fact. He has been raised to the
right side of God and received from him the Holy
Spirit, as his Father had promised; and what you now
see and hear is his gift that he has poured out on us.
For David himself did not go up into heaven; rather
he said: "The Lord said to my Lord: Sit here at my
right side, until I put your enemies as a footstool under
your feet." All the people of Israel, then, are to know
for sure that it is this Jesus, whom you nailed to the
cross, that God has made Lord and Messiah!

Response

The Lord is risen indeed, alleluia.
  Simon Peter has seen him, alleluia.

Canticle of Zachary   **See page 255**

Ant. The Son of Man must be handed over to sinful
        men,
        be nailed to the cross
        and be raised to life on the third day, alleluia.
        (Lk 24:7)

Morning Prayer

Almighty and everlasting God,
may we always serve your majesty
with wills devoted to your service
and in singleness of purpose.
Grant this through Christ our Lord.
  Amen.

Apostles' Creed   **Lord's Prayer**

The whole life of a saint is
  one mighty integrated prayer.

                                                    Origen

EASTER—Tuesday Evening

Christ is risen from the dead!
**He trampled down death by his death
and brought life to those in the grave.**

Psalm 76: Christ Is the Victor

Ant. Christ was raised from death by the glorious
power of the Father, alleluia. (Rom 6:4)

God is well known in Judah,
and famous in Israel.
He has his home in Jerusalem;
he lives on Mount Zion.
There he broke the arrows of the enemies,
their shields and swords, yes, all their weapons.

How glorious you are, God!
How majestic, as you return from the mountains
where you defeated your foes!
Their brave soldiers have been stripped of their loot,
and are now sleeping the sleep of death;
there is no one left to use their weapons.
When you threatened them, God of Jacob,
the horses and their riders fell dead.

But you—how men fear you!
Who can stand in your presence
when you are angry?
You made your judgment known from heaven;
the earth was afraid and lay still,
when you rose up to pronounce judgment,
to save all the oppressed on earth.

Men's anger only results in more praise for you;
those who survive the wars will keep your festivals.
Give the Lord your God what you promised him;
all you nearby nations bring gifts to him.

191

God makes men fear him;
   he humiliates proud princes,
   and terrorizes great kings.

Glory to the Father and to the Son and to the Holy
     Spirit;
   as in the beginning, so now, and for ever. Amen.

Ant. Christ was raised from death by the glorious
   power of the Father, alleluia.

Psalm Prayer

Let us pray (pause for silent prayer)
Lord Jesus Christ,
when you rose up from the grave,
the guards were so afraid they trembled
and became like dead men;
make us who believe and trust in your resurrection
confident of our victory over death and the grave
because of the glorious power of your Father.
You live and reign for ever and ever.
  Amen.

Reading   **1 Pt 1:18-21**

You know what was paid to set you free from the
worthless manner of life you received from your ancestors. It was not something that loses its value, such
as silver or gold; you were set free by the costly sacrifice of Christ, who was like a lamb without defect or
spot. He had been chosen by God before the creation
of the world, and was revealed in these last days for
your sake. Through him you believe in God, who
raised him from death and gave him glory; and so your
faith and hope are fixed on God.

Response

Just as Christ was raised from death, alleluia,
We also must live a new life, alleluia.

Canticle of Mary   **See page 256**

Ant. Stretch out your hand, Thomas,
        and put it in my side.
        Stop your doubting and believe, alleluia.
        (Jn 20:27)

Let Us Pray

Lord Jesus, Savior of the world, King of the new
        creation,
    Hear us, risen Lord.
Lord Jesus, always living in your Church,
    Hear us, risen Lord.
Lord Jesus, pouring out your Spirit on all mankind,
    Hear us, risen Lord.
Lord Jesus, comfort of the sick, the sorrowful and the
        dying,
    Hear us, risen Lord.
Lord Jesus, undying light of the faithful departed,
    Hear us, risen Lord.

(spontaneous prayer)

Evening Prayer

Lord our God,
preserve for us the grace of our baptism
and illuminate more fully
the eyes which you have opened for us.
We ask this through your only Son,
our Lord, God, King and Savior, Jesus Christ,
through whom and with whom
is praise, honor, glory, majesty and power

to the blessed Trinity,
both now and for ever.
   Amen.

Apostles' Creed   **Lord's Prayer**

Prayer does not blind us to the world,
   but it transforms our vision of the world,
   and makes us see it, all men,
   and all the history of mankind,
   in the light of God.

Thomas Merton

TO CHRIST OUR SOLE TEACHER

I render you thanks, Jesus,
that by your light I have come this far.
In your light I see the light of my life.
I see how you, the Word, infuse life into all
    believers,
and make perfect all who love you.
What teaching, good Jesus, was ever briefer
and more effectual than yours?
You persuade us to believe,
you bid us but to love.
What is easier than to believe in God?
What is sweeter than to love him?
How pleasant is your yoke, how light is your
    burden,
you, the one and only teacher!
To those who obey this teaching you promise
    all their desires,

for you require nothing that is difficult to a
  believer,
nothing that a lover can refuse.
Such are the promises that you make your
  disciples,
and they are entirely true,
for you are the truth, who can promise nothing
  but the truth.
Even more, it is none other than yourself that
  you promise,
who are the perfection of all that may be made
  perfect.
To you be praise,
to you be glory,
to you be rendered thanks
through endless ages! Amen.

Cardinal Nicholas of Cusa

Christ is risen, alleluia.
He is risen indeed, alleluia.
O Lord, open my lips.
And my mouth shall declare your praise.

Psalm 97: Give Thanks to Our Risen Lord

Ant. The earth sees and trembles at your resurrection,
O Lord.

The Lord is king! Be glad, earth!
Rejoice, all you islands of the seas!
Clouds and darkness are around him;
his kingdom is based on righteousness and justice.
Fire goes in front of him,
and burns up his enemies around him.
His lightning lights up the world;
the earth sees it and trembles.
The hills melt like wax before the Lord,
before the Lord of all the earth.
The heavens proclaim his righteousness,
and all peoples see his glory.

All who worship images are ashamed,
all who boast of their idols;
all the gods bow down before him.
The people of Zion are glad,
and the cities of Judah rejoice,
because of your judgments, Lord!
Lord Almighty, you are ruler of all the earth;
you are much greater than all the gods.

The Lord loves those who hate evil;
he protects the lives of his people,
he rescues them from the power of the wicked.
Light shines on the righteous,
and gladness on the good.

All you that are righteous, be glad,
   because of what the Lord has done!
Remember what the Holy One has done,
   and give thanks to him!

Glory to the Father and to the Son and to the Holy
    Spirit;
   as in the beginning, so now, and for ever. Amen.

Ant. The earth sees and trembles at your resurrection,
   O Lord.

Psalm Prayer

Let us pray (pause for silent prayer)
Holy God and Father,
you rescue those who hate evil
from the power of the wicked and the godless.
Build your kingdom of righteousness among men
and light up the world with the long-awaited coming
of our Lord Jesus Christ,
who lives and reigns with you and the Holy Spirit,
one God, for ever and ever.
   Amen.

Reading   **Acts 3:13-15**

The God of Abraham, Isaac, and Jacob, the God of
our ancestors, has given divine glory to his Servant
Jesus. You handed him over to the authorities, and
you rejected him in Pilate's presence, even after Pilate
had decided to set him free. He was holy and good,
but you rejected him and instead you asked Pilate to do
you the favor of turning loose a murderer. And so you
killed the Author of life. But God raised him from the
dead—and we are witnesses to this.

Response

Thanks be to God who gives us the victory, alleluia.
   Through our Lord Jesus Christ, alleluia.

Canticle of Zachary   **See page 255**

Ant. The Messiah had to suffer
         and be raised from death on the third day,
         alleluia. (Lk 24:46)

Morning Prayer

Creator and Savior of the human race,
worthy of all praise and thanksgiving,
you have established your Church
on the rock of faith in your risen Son.
Free us from our enemies, seen and unseen,
and unite us in the bonds of peace and brotherhood.
Grant this through Christ our Lord.
   Amen.

Apostles' Creed   **Lord's Prayer**

Our Father is good,
And we have received from him
   the spirit of adoption.
When we ask him for food he gives us living bread,
   and not a stone.
What the Father gives is good;
When we ask him for his gifts,
He showers them down on us from heaven.
                    Origen of Alexandria

EASTER—Wednesday Evening

Christ is risen from the dead!
  He trampled down death by his death
    and brought life to those in the grave.

Psalm 103: The Rich Kindness of God

Ant. Be merciful, just as your Father is merciful,
      alleluia. (Lk 6:36)

Praise the Lord, my soul!
  All my being, praise his holy name!
Praise the Lord, my soul,
  and do not forget how kind he is.
He forgives all my sins
  and heals all my diseases;
he saves me from the grave
  and blesses me with love and mercy;
he fills my life with good things,
  so that I stay young and strong like an eagle.

The Lord judges in favor of the oppressed
  and gives them their rights.
He told his plans to Moses
  and let the people of Israel see his mighty acts.
The Lord is merciful and loving,
  slow to become angry, and full of constant love.
He does not keep on reprimanding;
  he is not angry forever.
He does not punish us as we deserve,
  or repay us for our sins and wrongs.
As high as the sky is above the earth,
  so great is his love for those who fear him.

As far as the east is from the west,
  so far does he remove our sins from us.
As kind as a father is to his children,
  so the Lord is kind to those who fear him.

He knows what we are made of;
  he remembers that we are dust.

As for man, his life is like grass;
  he grows and flourishes like a wild flower.
Then the wind blows on it, and it is gone,
  and no one sees it again.
But the Lord's love for those who honor him lasts
      forever,
  and his goodness endures for all generations,
to those who are true to his covenant,
  and who faithfully obey his commandments.

The Lord set up his throne in heaven;
  he is king over all.
Praise the Lord, you strong and mighty angels,
  who obey his commands,
  who listen to what he says!
Praise the Lord, all you heavenly powers,
  you servants who do what he wants!
Praise the Lord, all his creatures,
  in every place he rules!
  Praise the Lord, my soul!

Glory to the Father and to the Son and to the Holy
      Spirit;
  as in the beginning, so now, and for ever. Amen.

Ant. Be merciful, just as your Father is merciful,
      alleluia.

Psalm Prayer

Let us pray (pause for silent prayer)
Merciful and loving Father,
you saved your only Son from the grave
and made him the source of salvation for all who
  believe;

forgive our sins,
heal all our diseases, and save all the oppressed of the
     earth.
We ask this through Christ our Lord.
   Amen.

Reading   1 Pt 2:4-5

Come to the Lord, the living stone rejected as worthless by men, but chosen as valuable by God. Come as
living stones, and let yourselves be used in building
the spiritual temple, where you will serve as holy
priests, to offer spiritual and acceptable sacrifices to
God through Jesus Christ.

Response

If we have died with Christ, alleluia.
   We believe we will also live with him, alleluia.

Canticle of Mary   **See page 256**

Ant. Thomas answered Jesus:
       My Lord and my God, alleluia. (Jn 20:28)

Let Us Pray

Lord Jesus, light and salvation of all nations,
   Hear us, risen Lord.
Lord Jesus, always standing and interceding for us,
   Hear us, risen Lord.
Lord Jesus, the same yesterday, today and for ever,
   Hear us, risen Lord.
Lord Jesus, consolation of the persecuted and afflicted,
   Hear us, risen Lord.
Lord Jesus, light and peace for our beloved dead,
   Hear us, risen Lord.

(spontaneous prayer)

Evening Prayer

O Shepherd of Israel,
you rescued your Son, our Savior,
from the death-dark valley
and anointed him as Messiah and Lord.
Grant that we may drink
*   from the overflowing cup of his Spirit*
and dwell in your house all the days of our life.
We ask this through Jesus our Lord.
   Amen.

Apostles' Creed   **Lord's Prayer**

The glory of God is a human person fully alive
   and the life of such a person
   consists in beholding God.
                         St. Irenaeus of Lyons

THE GLORIOUS MYSTERIES OF THE ROSARY

1. Hail Mary . . . and blessed is the fruit of your womb, Jesus,
   who rose from the dead on the third day.
2. Hail Mary . . . and blessed is the fruit of your womb, Jesus,
   who ascended into heaven to sit at the Father's right hand.
3. Hail Mary. . . and blessed is the fruit of your womb, Jesus,
   who promised us the Holy Spirit.
4. Hail Mary . . . and blessed is the fruit of your womb, Jesus,
   who took you up, body and soul, into heaven.
5. Hail Mary . . . and blessed is the fruit of your womb, Jesus,
   who crowned you Queen of Heaven.

O God,
   your only-begotten Son won for us the rewards of eternal salvation
by his life, death and resurrection.
As we meditate on these mysteries
   of the rosary of the Blessed Virgin Mary,
may we imitate what they contain
and receive what they so graciously promise.
We ask this through the same Christ our Lord.
Amen.

EASTER—Thursday Morning

Christ is risen, alleluia.
He is risen indeed, alleluia.
O Lord, open my lips.
And my mouth shall declare your praise.

Psalm 24[b]: Christ's Triumphant Entry into Heaven

Ant. He ascended into heaven and is seated at the right hand of the Father. (Creed)

Fling wide the gates,
  open the ancient doors,
  and the king of glory will enter in!

Who is this great king of glory?

He is the Lord Christ, strong and mighty,
  the Lord Jesus, victorious in battle.
Fling wide the gates,
  open the ancient doors,
  and the king of glory will enter in!

Who is this great king of glory?

He is the Lord Christ, strong and mighty,
  the Lord Jesus, victorious in battle.
Fling wide the gates,
  open the ancient doors,
  and the king of glory will enter in!

Who is this great king of glory?

The Lord of armies, he is the great king of glory!

Glory to the Father and to the Son and to the Holy Spirit;
  as in the beginning, so now, and for ever. Amen.

Ant. He ascended into heaven and is seated at the right hand of the Father.

Psalm Prayer

Let us pray (pause for silent prayer)
Lord Jesus Christ, king of glory,
seated at the right hand of your Father,
bring your people in triumphal procession
into the kingdom of heaven,
where you live and reign for ever and ever.
   Amen.

Reading   **Acts 1:6-11**

When the apostles met together with Jesus they asked him, "Lord, will you at this time give the Kingdom back to Israel?" Jesus said to them: "The times and occasions are set by my Father's own authority, and it is not for you to know when they will be. But you will be filled with power when the Holy Spirit comes on you, and you will be witnesses for me in Jerusalem, in all of Judea and Samaria, and to the ends of the earth." After saying this, he was taken up into heaven as they watched him, and a cloud hid him from their sight.

   They still had their eyes fixed on the sky as he went away, when two men dressed in white suddenly stood beside them. "Men of Galilee," they said, "why do you stand there looking up at the sky? This Jesus, who was taken up from you into heaven, will come back in the same way that you saw him go to heaven."

Response

Freedom is what we have, alleluia.
   Christ has set us free, alleluia.

Canticle of Zachary   **See page 255**

Ant. I have been given all authority in heaven and on
         earth.
         Go, then, to all peoples everywhere
         and make them my disciples, alleluia.
         (Mt 28:18-19)

Morning Prayer

O King of glory and Lord of hosts,
who ascended triumphantly above all the heavens,
do not leave us orphans.
but send us the Promised of the Father,
the Spirit of truth.
Blessed be the holy and undivided Trinity now and
   for ever.
   Amen.

Apostles' Creed   **Lord's Prayer**

As you covet to be God's lover,
   love his name JESUS, and think it in your heart,
   so that you never forget it wherever you are.
                                        Richard Rolle

EASTER—Thursday Evening

Christ is risen from the dead!
**He trampled down death by his death
and brought life to those in the grave.**

Psalm 47: Christ's Glorious Ascension

Ant. Christ went up, above and beyond the heavens,
to fill the whole universe with his presence,
alleluia. (Eph 4:10)

Clap your hands for joy, all peoples!
Praise God with loud songs!
The Lord, the Most High, is to be feared;
he is a great king, ruling over all the world.
He gave us victory over the peoples;
he made us rule over the nations.
He chose for us the land where we live,
the proud possession of his people, whom he loves.

God goes up to his throne!
There are shouts of joy and the blast of trumpets,
as the Lord goes up!
Sing praise to God;
sing praise to our king!
God is king over all the world;
praise him with songs!

God sits on his sacred throne;
he rules over the nations.
The rulers of the nations come together
with the people of the God of Abraham.
The shields of all the warriors belong to God;
he rules over all!

Glory to the Father and to the Son and to the Holy
Spirit;
as in the beginning, so now, and for ever. Amen.

Ant. Christ went up, above and beyond the heavens,
to fill the whole universe with his presence,
alleluia.

Psalm Prayer

Let us pray (pause for silent prayer)
Almighty and everlasting God,
grant that we who believe that your only-begotten Son
ascended into heaven and now sits at your right hand,
may ourselves dwell in spirit amid heavenly things.
We ask this through the same Christ our Lord.
   Amen.

Reading   **1 Pt 2:24-25**

Christ himself carried our sins on his body to the cross,
so that we might die to sin and live for righteousness.
By his wounds you have been healed. You were like
sheep that had lost their way; but now you have been
brought back to follow the Shepherd and Keeper of
your souls.

Response

You are to think of yourselves as dead to sin, alleluia.
   But alive to God in union with Christ Jesus, alleluia.

Canticle of Mary   **See page 256**

Ant. I go back up to him who is my Father and your
Father, my God and your God, alleluia.
(Jn 20:17)

Let Us Pray

Lord Jesus, King of glory, sitting at the right hand of
the Father,
  Hear us, risen Lord.
Lord Jesus, filling the whole universe with your
presence,
  Hear us, risen Lord.
Lord Jesus, drawing all things to yourself,
  Hear us, risen Lord.
Lord Jesus, who will come again to judge the living
and the dead,
  Hear us, risen Lord.
Lord Jesus, who promised the gift of the Spirit of truth,
  Hear us, risen Lord.

(spontaneous prayer)

Evening Prayer

God of salvation,
you heard your Son when he cried to you
from the midst of his foes,
and raised him up out of the sleep of death.
Shield us from our enemies
and bring us home in safety to your holy mountain.
Grant this through Christ our Lord.
  Amen.

Apostles' Creed   **Lord's Prayer**

TO THE SACRED HEART OF JESUS

May the heart of Jesus in the most blessed
    sacrament of the altar
  be praised, adored and loved,
  with grateful affection, at every moment,
  even unto the end of time.

Learn from me for I am meek and humble of
    heart;
  And you will find rest for your souls.

O God, our loving Father,
  you graciously grant us the inexhaustible
    treasures of love
    contained in the heart of Jesus, your Son.
  Grant that by paying him true and loving
    service
  we may offer fitting reparation to this heart
    wounded by our sins.
We ask this through the same Christ our Lord.
Amen.

EASTER—Friday Morning

Christ is risen, alleluia.
He is risen indeed, alleluia.
O Lord, open my lips.
And my mouth shall declare your praise.

Psalm 135: God Creates a People for Himself

Ant. You are God's own people, alleluia. (1 Pt 2:9)

Praise his name, you servants of the Lord,
   who stand in the Lord's house,
   in the sanctuary of our God.
Praise the Lord, because he is good;
   sing praises to his name, because he is kind.
He chose Jacob for himself,
   the people of Israel for his own.

I know that our Lord is great;
   he is greater than all the gods.
He does whatever he wishes
   in heaven and on earth,
   in the seas and in the depths below.
He brings storm clouds from the ends of the earth;
   he makes lightning for the storms,
   and brings out the wind from his storeroom.

In Egypt he killed all the firstborn
   of both men and animals.
There he performed miracles and wonders
   to punish Pharaoh and all his officials.
He destroyed many nations,
   and killed powerful kings:
   all the kings in Canaan.
He gave their land to his people;
   he gave it to Israel.

Lord, men will always know that you are God;
   all generations will remember you.

The Lord will take pity on his people;
  he will set his servants free.

Glory to the Father and to the Son and to the Holy
    Spirit;
  as in the beginning, so now, and for ever. Amen.

Ant. You are God's own people, alleluia.

Psalm Prayer

Let us pray (pause for silent prayer)
Merciful and loving Father,
you saved your only Son from the grave
and made him the source of salvation for all who
    believe.
Forgive us our sins,
heal all our diseases
and rescue the oppressed of the earth
from their tormentors.
We ask this through Christ our Lord.
  Amen.

Reading   **Acts 5: 30-32**

The God of our fathers raised Jesus from death, after
you had killed him by nailing him to a cross. And God
raised him to his right side as Leader and Savior, to
give to the people of Israel the opportunity to repent
and have their sins forgiven. We are witnesses to these
things—we and the Holy Spirit, who is God's gift to
those who obey him.

Response

God raised Christ from the dead, alleluia.
  He set him free from the pains of death, alleluia.

Canticle of Zachary   **See page 255**

Ant. Remember! I will be with you always,
        to the end of the age, alleluia. (Mt 28:20)

Morning Prayer

*Almighty and everlasting God,
grant that we who believe
that your only-begotten Son, our Savior,
rose from the dead and ascended into heaven,
may ourselves dwell in spirit amid heavenly things.
We ask this through the same Christ our Lord.*
   Amen.

Apostles' Creed   **Lord's Prayer**

**It is not enough to leave Egypt,
   one must also enter the Promised Land.**
                                    St. John Chrysostom

EASTER—Friday Evening

Christ is risen from the dead!
**He trampled down death by his death
and brought life to those in the grave.**

Psalm 136: God's Love Is Eternal

Give thanks to the Lord, because he is good,
And his love is eternal.
Give thanks to the greatest of all gods;
His love is eternal.
Give thanks to the mightiest of all lords;
His love is eternal.

He alone does great miracles;
His love is eternal.
By his wisdom he made the heavens;
His love is eternal;
he built the earth on the deep waters;
His love is eternal.
He made the sun and the moon;
His love is eternal;
the sun to rule over the day;
His love is eternal;
the moon and the stars to rule over the night;
His love is eternal.

He killed the firstborn sons of the Egyptians;
His love is eternal.
He led the people of Israel out of Egypt;
His love is eternal;
with his strong hand, his powerful arm;
His love is eternal.
He divided the Sea of Reeds;
His love is eternal;
he led his people through it;
His love is eternal;
he drowned Pharaoh and his army;
His love is eternal.

He led his people in the desert;
His love is eternal.
He killed powerful kings;
His love is eternal;
he killed famous kings;
His love is eternal.
He gave their land to his people;
His love is eternal;
he gave it to Israel, his servant;
His love is eternal.

He did not forget us when we were defeated;
His love is eternal;
he freed us from our enemies;
His love is eternal.
He gives food to all men and animals;
His love is eternal.

Give thanks to the God of heaven;
His love is eternal.

Glory to the Father and to the Son and to the Holy
    Spirit;
  as in the beginning, so now, and for ever. Amen.

Psalm Prayer

Let us pray (pause for silent prayer)
Creator and Savior of the human race,
worthy of all praise and thanksgiving,
establish your Church on the bedrock of faith,
free us from our enemies, seen and unseen,
and unite us in the bonds of peace and brotherhood.
We ask this through Christ our Lord.
  Amen.

Reading   **1 Pt 3:18-19**

Christ himself died for you; once and for all he died for sins, a good man for bad men, in order to lead you to God. He was put to death physically, but made alive spiritually; and in his spiritual existence he went and preached to the imprisoned spirits.

Response

Christ was shown with great power to be the Son of
      God, alleluia.
   By being raised from the dead, alleluia.

Canticle of Mary   **See page 256**

Ant. Look at my hands and my feet
         and see that it is I, myself, alleluia.
         (Lk 24:39)

Let Us Pray

Lord Jesus, victorious King, crush beneath your feet
      the prince of darkness and his powers.
   Hear us, risen Lord.
Lord Jesus, grant us victory over the temptations of
      our visible and invisible enemies.
   Hear us, risen Lord.
Lord Jesus, make us rise from the tomb of our sins
      and offenses.
   Hear us, risen Lord.
Lord Jesus, fill us with the joy and happiness of your
      resurrection.
   Hear us, risen Lord.
Lord Jesus, conduct us to the divine wedding feast to
      rejoice with all the saints.
   Hear us, risen Lord.

(spontaneous prayer)

Evening Prayer

Risen Lord,
whose power is beyond compare
and whose love for mankind is beyond words to
*   describe,*
hear the prayers of your ransomed people
and grant us the riches of your promised mercy;
for you are our light and our resurrection,
O Christ our God,
and we glorify you, and your eternal Father
and your holy and life-giving Spirit,
now and for ever.
Amen.

Apostles' Creed   **Lord's Prayer**

Let us fix our eyes on the blood of Christ
**   and let us realize how precious it is to the Father,**
**   since it was poured out for our salvation**
**   and brought the grace of**
**   repentance to the whole world.**
St. Clement of Rome

THE VICTORIOUS CROSS

We adore you, Lord Jesus Christ, as you ascend
your cross.
May this cross deliver us from the destroying
angel.

We adore your wounded body as it hangs on
the cross.
May your wounds be our healing.

We adore you dead and buried in the tomb.
May your death be our life.

We adore you as you descend among the dead
to deliver them.
May we never hear the dread sentence of
doom.

We adore you rising from the dead.
Free us from the weight of our sins.

We adore you ascending to the right hand of
   God your Father.
   Raise us to eternal glory along with all your
   saints.

We adore you as you come to judge the living
   and the dead.
   At your coming be not our Judge but our
   Savior.

Holy Cross,
   You are more exalted than all the trees of
   the forest:
   on you hung the life of the world;
   on you Christ proceeded to his triumph;
   on you death overcame death.

Holy God, Holy Mighty One, Holy Immortal
   One:
   who take away the sins of the world,
   have mercy on us.

   From a tenth-century manuscript

EASTER—Saturday Morning

Christ is risen, alleluia.
He is risen indeed, alleluia.
O Lord, open my lips.
And my mouth shall declare your praise.

Psalm 82: Christ the Supreme Ruler

Ant. Holy is God, holy and mighty, holy and living
for ever, alleluia.

God presides in the heavenly council;
in the meeting of the gods he gives his decision:
"Defend the rights of the poor and the orphans;
be fair to the needy and the helpless.
Rescue the poor and the needy;
save them from the power of evil men!

"How ignorant you are, how stupid!
You live in darkness,
and justice has disappeared from the world.
I told you that you are gods,
that all of you are sons of the Most High.
But you will die like men;
your life will end like any prince."

Come, God, and rule the world;
all the nations are yours.

Glory to the Father and to the Son and to the Holy
Spirit;
as in the beginning, so now, and for ever. Amen.

Ant. Holy is God, holy and mighty, holy and living for
ever, alleluia.

Psalm Prayer

Let us pray (pause for silent prayer)
Almighty God, Father of our Lord Jesus Christ,
you have brought us to new birth
by water and the Holy Spirit
and forgiven all our sins.
Anoint us with your Holy Spirit,
perfect us with his sevenfold gifts
and establish us in justice and in peace.
Grant this through Jesus Christ our Lord.
    Amen.

Reading   **Acts 10:40-43**

God raised Jesus from death on the third day, and
caused him to appear. He was not seen by all the
people, but only by us who are the witnesses that God
had already chosen. We ate and drank with him after
God raised him from death. And he commanded us to
preach the gospel to the people, and to testify that he
is the one whom God has appointed Judge of the living
and the dead. All the prophets spoke about him, saying that everyone who believes in him will have his
sins forgiven through the power of his name.

Response

I see heaven opened, alleluia.
    And the Son of Man standing at the right hand of
    God, alleluia.

Canticle of Zachary   **See page 255**

Ant. After the Lord Jesus had talked with them,
        he was taken up to heaven
        and sat at the right side of God, alleluia.
        (Mk 16:19)

Morning Prayer

God our Father,
in whom the hearts and minds of the faithful are
    united,
help us to love your commandments
and to yearn after your promises,
so that amid the changing circumstances of this life
our hearts may be fixed where true joys abound.
We ask this through Christ our Lord.
    Amen.

Apostles' Creed   **Lord's Prayer**

We must serve God as he wishes,
    not as we choose.

                          St. Teresa of Avila

EASTER—Saturday Evening

Christ is risen from the dead!
**He trampled down death by his death
and brought life to those in the grave.**

Easter Anthem: (1 Cor 5:7-8; Rom 6:9-11,
1 Cor 15:20-22)

Ant. Alleluia, alleluia, alleluia!

Our Passover feast is ready
  now that Christ, our Passover lamb, has been
    sacrificed.
Let us celebrate our feast, then,
  not with bread having the old yeast,
  the yeast of sin and immorality,
but with the bread that has no yeast,
  the bread of purity and truth.

For we know that Christ has been raised from death
  and will never die again—
  death has no power over him.
The death he died was death to sin, once and for all;
  and the life he now lives is life to God.
In the same way you are to think of yourselves as dead
    to sin
  but alive to God in union with Christ Jesus.

Christ has been raised from death,
  as the guarantee that those who sleep in death will
    also be raised.
For just as death came by means of a man,
  in the same way the rising from death comes by
    means of a man.
For just as all men die because of their union with
    Adam
  in the same way all will be raised to life because of
    their union to Christ.

Glory to the Father and to the Son and to the Holy
    Spirit;
  as in the beginning, so now, and for ever. Amen.

Ant. Alleluia, alleluia, alleluia!

Collect Prayer

Let us pray (pause for silent prayer)
Lord Jesus
may we who celebrate the mysteries
of your passion, death and resurrection
rejoice together with all your saints
when you come again in glory
to judge the living and the dead.
You live and reign for ever and ever.
    Amen.

Reading   **Heb 5:7-9**

In his life on earth Jesus made his prayers and requests
with loud cries and tears to God, who could save him
from death. Because he was humble and devoted, God
heard him. But even though he was God's Son he
learned to be obedient by means of his sufferings.
When he was made perfect, he became the source of
eternal salvation for all those who obey him.

Response

Christ, our Passover lamb, has been sacrificed, alleluia.
    Let us celebrate our feast, alleluia.

Canticle of Mary   **See page 256**

Ant. For forty days after his death Jesus showed him-
    self to his apostles many times, alleluia. (Acts
    1:3)

Let Us Pray

Lord Jesus, high priest of the new and eternal covenant,
   Hear us, risen Lord.
Lord Jesus, victor over death and hell,
   Hear us, risen Lord.
Lord Jesus, purifying and strengthening your Church
    by the Spirit,
   Hear us, risen Lord.
Lord Jesus, the beginning and the end of God's plan,
   Hear us, risen Lord.
Lord Jesus, the life and hope of those who die in you,
   Hear us, risen Lord.

(spontaneous prayer)

Evening Prayer

Heavenly Father,
you raised Jesus Christ from the dead
and made him sit at your right hand.
Rescue us from our sins,
bring us to new life in him,
raise us up with him,
and give us a place with him in heaven,
in the same Christ Jesus our Lord.
   Amen.

Apostles' Creed   **Lord's Prayer**

HYMN TO THE HOLY SPIRIT

O Holy Spirit, by whose breath
  Life rises vibrant out of death:
  Come to create, renew, inspire;
  Come, kindle in our hearts your fire.

You are the seeker's sure resource,
  Of burning love the living source,
  Protector in the midst of strife,
  The giver and the Lord of life.

In you God's energy is shown,
  To us your varied gifts made known.
  Teach us to speak, teach us to hear;
  Yours is the tongue and yours the ear.

Flood our dull senses with your light;
  In mutual love our hearts unite.
  Your power the whole creation fills;
  Confirm our weak, uncertain wills.

From inner strife grant us release;
  Turn nations to the ways of peace,
  To fuller life your people bring
  That as one body we may sing:

Praise to the Father, Christ his Word,
  And to the Spirit, God the Lord;
  To them all honor, glory be
  Both now and for eternity.
Amen.

PENTECOST

PENTECOST—Morning

Blessed be the Father, the Son and the Holy Spirit
who enlighten and sanctify our souls and bodies
at all times.
Now and always and for ever and ever. Amen.
O Lord, open my lips.
And my mouth shall declare your praise.

Psalm 104: The New Creation

Ant. When you give them breath, they live; you give
new life to the earth, alleluia.

Praise the Lord, my soul!
Lord, my God, how great you are!
You are clothed with majesty and glory;
you cover yourself with light.
You stretched out the heavens like a tent,
and built your home on the waters above.
You use the clouds as your chariot,
and walk on the wings of the wind.
You use the winds as your messengers,
and flashes of lightning as your servants.

From heaven you send rain on the mountains,
and the earth is filled with your blessings.
You make grass grow for the cattle,
and plants for man to use,
so he can grow his crops,
and produce wine to make him happy,
olive oil to make him cheerful,
and bread to give him strength.

Lord, you have made so many things!
How wisely you made them all!
The earth is filled with your creatures.
All of them depend on you,
to give them food when they need it.

You give it to them, and they eat it;
  you provide food, and they are satisfied.
When you turn away, they are afraid;
  when you hold back your breath, they die,
  and go back to the soil they came from.

But when you give them breath, they live;
  you give new life to the earth.
May the glory of the Lord last forever!
  May the Lord be happy with what he made!
I will sing to the Lord all my life;
  I will sing praises to my God as long as I live.

Glory to the Father and to the Son and to the Holy
      Spirit;
  as in the beginning, so now, and for ever. Amen.

Ant. When you give them breath, they live; you give
      new life to the earth, alleluia.

Psalm Prayer

Let us pray (pause for silent prayer)
O God, on the first Pentecost,
you instructed the hearts of those who believed in you
by the light of the Holy Spirit;
under the inspiration of the same Spirit
give us a taste for what is right and true
and a continuing sense of his joy-bringing presence
and power.
We ask this through Jesus Christ our Lord.
  Amen.

Reading   Acts 5:30-32

The God of our fathers raised Jesus from death, after
you had killed him by nailing him to a cross. And
God raised him to his right side as Leader and Savior,
to give to the people of Israel the opportunity to repent

and have their sins forgiven. We are witnesses to these things—we and the Holy Spirit, who is God's gift to those who obey him.

Response

They were all filled with the Holy Spirit, alleluia.
And began to speak as the Spirit gave them utterance, alleluia.

Canticle of Zachary   **See page 255**

Ant. Receive the Holy Spirit.
        If you forgive men's sins
        then they are forgiven, alleluia.
        (Jn 20:22-23)

Morning Prayer

In loving gratitude, Father,
for all that you have accomplished for us
in and through Jesus, your Son and our Brother,
we pray for the fullness of the gifts of the Spirit,
that we may praise you as we ought
—even with sighs and groans unutterable—
as we await the full outcome of your divine purposes.
Grant that we may sing to you with spiritual desire
and be admitted among the heavenly choirs
to rejoice before you with all your saints,
for ever and ever.
    Amen.

Apostles' Creed   **Lord's Prayer**

It is through the gift of the Holy Spirit that man comes by faith to the contemplation and appreciation of the divine plan.
    Constitution on the Church in the Modern World

PENTECOST—Evening

Christ is risen from the dead!
He trampled down death by his death
and brought life to those in the grave.

Psalm 29

Ant. Each person there was touched by a tongue of
fire, alleluia. (Acts 2:3)

Praise the Lord, you gods;
    praise his glory and power.
Praise the Lord's glorious name,
    bow down before the Holy One when he appears.

The Lord's voice is heard on the seas;
    the glorious God thunders,
    and his voice echoes over the ocean.
The Lord's voice is heard
    in all its might and majesty.

The Lord's voice breaks the cedars,
    even the cedars of Lebanon.
He causes the mountains of Lebanon to jump like
        calves,
    and Mount Hermon to leap like a young bull.

The Lord's voice makes the lightning flash.
    His voice makes the desert shake;
    he shakes the desert of Kadesh.
The Lord's voice makes the deer give birth,
    and leaves the trees stripped bare,
    while in his temple all shout, "Glory to God!"

The Lord rules over the deep waters;
    he rules as king forever.
The Lord gives strength to his people,
    and blesses them with peace.

Glory to the Father and to the Son and to the Holy
    Spirit;
    as in the beginning, so now, and for ever. Amen.

Ant. Each person there was touched by a tongue of
    fire, alleluia.

Psalm Prayer

Let us pray (pause for silent prayer)
Lord God of all creation,
in the beginning your Spirit brooded over the waters
and brought forth a world of bounty and of beauty.
In these final days may the same Creator Spirit
come to create and inspire us anew
until the whole world can sing with us,
"Glory to God!"
We ask this through Jesus our Lord.
    Amen.

Reading   **Rom 8:11**

If the Spirit of God, who raised Jesus from death, lives
in you, then he who raised Christ from death will also
give life to your mortal bodies by the presence of his
Spirit in you.

Response

The Holy Spirit, the Paraclete, will teach you all things,
    alleluia.
    And lead you into all truth, alleluia.

Canticle of Mary   **See page 256**

Ant. Come, Holy Spirit, fill the hearts of your faithful
    and kindle in them the fire of your divine love,
    alleluia.

Let Us Pray

Lord and life-giving Spirit, you brooded over the
  primeval waters.
  Come, fill our hearts.
You led your people out of slavery and into the free-
  dom of the children of God.
  Come, fill our hearts.
You overshadowed Mary of Nazareth and made her
  the Mother of God.
  Come, fill our hearts.
You anointed Jesus as Messiah when he was baptized
  by John in the Jordan.
  Come, fill our hearts.
You raised Jesus out of death and proclaimed him Son
  of God in all his power.
  Come, fill our hearts.
You appeared in tongues of flame on Pentecost and
  endowed your Church with charismatic gifts.
  Come, fill our hearts.
You send us out to testify to the Good News about
  Jesus Christ.
  Come, fill our hearts.

(spontaneous prayer)

Evening Prayer

Heavenly King, Consoler, Spirit of truth,
present in all places and filling all things,
treasury of blessings and giver of life:

come and dwell in us,
cleanse us of every stain of sin,
and save our souls,
O gracious Lord,
living and reigning with the eternal Father
and his only-begotten and beloved Son,
one Holy Trinity, for ever and ever.
   Amen.

Apostles' Creed   **Lord's Prayer**

Do not set your heart on what seems good to you
   but rather on what is pleasing
   to God when you pray.
   This will free you from disturbance
   and leave you occupied with
   thanksgiving in your prayer.

                              Evagrius of Pontus

DOXOLOGY

Blessing and honor and thanksgiving and
    praise,
more than we can utter, more than we can
    conceive,
be yours,
O holy and glorious Trinity, Father, Son and
    Holy Spirit,
by all angels, all men, all creatures,
for ever and ever.
Amen.

Bishop Thomas Ken

APPENDIX

Appendix

THE JESUS PRAYER

One of the oldest, simplest and best of prayers is a calling in faith upon the Holy Name of Jesus. By repeatedly invoking the proper name of Our Lord, God and Savior, Jesus Christ, Christians are convinced that they will be enabled to penetrate more and more deeply and surely into a growing awareness of the presence of God that saves and sanctifies. The sacred name is sometimes repeated by itself or sometimes inserted in a phrase. The common form of the fuller invocation is:

LORD JESUS CHRIST,
 SON OF THE LIVING GOD,
 HAVE MERCY ON ME, A SINNER.

The best way to say the Jesus Prayer is to sit in as much physical and inner stillness as one can manage and to repeat the invocation over and over, slowly and insistently, fixing the mind directly and intensely on the words of the prayer itself, without trying to conjure up any mental pictures or intellectual concepts. One should pray in this way without strain but with real effort for some length of time at each attempt. A rosary is a useful timer and reminder in this effort. Persistent, frequent attempts to pray in this way will gradually habituate the soul to more effortless and continuous use of the Divine Name until it becomes the very substance of one's life of prayer. It is well to use the Holy Name insistently and quietly before and after other forms of prayer. It can also be used during normal intervals in the day's work, when walking from place to place, and so forth, even when conditions are not ideal for recollected forms of prayer.

Great saints and fervent mystics tell us that the Jesus Prayer can even become self-acting as it descends from the lips and mind into the heart, the very center of a person's being. Such a gift comes as a pure grace, but as one that can and should be prepared for by genuine effort and serious habituation in the first place.

The Jesus Prayer is a high act of faith and self-surrender to the indwelling Spirit who longs to teach us to pray without ceasing to Abba, our Heavenly Father. It is a sure path to contemplative prayer and to "the peace which passes all understanding."

Jesus is honey to the mouth,
music to the ear,
a shout of gladness in the heart.
St. Bernard of Clairvaux

Table of Scripture Readings

Advent

	Year 1	Year 2

ADVENT SEASON TO 16 DECEMBER

Week I

	Year 1	Year 2
Sunday	Is 6:1-13	Is 1:1-18
Monday	Is 7:1-17	Is 1:21-2:5
Tuesday	Is 8:1-18	Is 2:6-22; 4:2-6
Wednesday	Is 9:1b-7	Is 5:1-7
Thursday	Is 10:5-21	Is 16:1-5; 17:4-8
Friday	Is 11:10-16	Is 19:16-25
Saturday	Is 13:1-22a	Is 21:6-12

Week II

	Year 1	Year 2
Sunday	Is 14:1-21	Is 22:8b-23
Monday	Is 34:1-17	Is 24:1-18a
Tuesday	Is 35:1-10	Is 24:18b-25:5
Wednesday	Ru 1:1-22	Is 25:6-26:6
Thursday	Ru 2:1-13	Is 26:7-21
Friday	Ru 2:14-23	Is 27:1-13
Saturday	Ru 3:1-18	Is 29:1-8

Week III

	Year 1	Year 2
Sunday	Ru 4:1-22	Is 29:13-24
Monday	1 Chr 17:1-15	Is 30:18-26
Tuesday	Mi 4:1-7	Is 30:27-31:9
Wednesday	Mi 5:1-8	Is 32:1-8
Thursday	Mi 7:7-13	Is 32:9-33:6
Friday	Mi 7:14-20	Is 33:7-24

FROM 17-24 DECEMBER

	Year 1	Year 2
Dec. 17	Is 40:1-11	Is 45:1-13
Dec. 18	Is 40:12-18, 21-31	Is 46:1-13
Dec. 19	Is 41:8-20	Is 47:1-15
Dec. 20	Is 41:21-29	Is 48:1-11
Dec. 21	Is 42:10-25	Is 48:12-21; 49:9b-13
Dec. 22	Is 43:1-13	Is 49:14-50:1
Dec. 23	Is 43:19-28	Is 51:1-11
Dec. 24	Is 44:1-8, 21-23	Is 51:17-52:10

Christmastide

Dec. 25   The Nativity of our Lord   Is 11:1-10

Sunday within the Octave of Christmas: Feast of the
   Holy Family   Eph 5:21-6:4

Dec. 26   Stephen the Protomartyr   Acts 6:8-7:2,
                                  44-59

Dec. 27   John, Apostle and Evang.   1 Jn. 1:1-2:3

Dec. 28   The Holy Innocents   Ex 1:8-16, 22

	Year 1	Year 2
Dec. 29	Col 1:1-14	Sg 1:1-8
Dec. 30	Col 1:15-2:3	Sg 1:9-2:7
Dec. 31	Col 2:4-15	Sg 2:8-3:5

Jan. 1   Solemnity of Mary Mother of God Heb 2:9-
                                        17

Jan. 2   Col 2:16-3:4   Sg 4:1-5:1

*In places where the Epiphany is celebrated on the
Sunday occurring between 2-8 January, the readings
given for 7-12 January are read after the Epiphany,
the following being omitted:*

Jan. 3   Col 3:5-16   Sg 5:2-6:2
Jan. 4   Col 3:17-4:1   Sg 6:3-7:10
Jan. 5   Col 4:2-18   Sg 7:11-8:7
Jan. 6   (*in places where the Epiphany is celebrated on
   Jan. 7 or 8*)
         Is 42:1-8   Is 49:1-9
Jan. 7   (*in places where the Epiphany is celebrated on
   Jan. 7 or 8*)
         Is 61:1-11   Is 54:1-17
Jan. 6   The Epiphany of our Lord   Is 60:1-22

*The readings assigned to 7-12 January are read on the
days which follow the solemnity of the Epiphany, even
when this is kept on the Sunday, until the following
Saturday. From the Monday after the Sunday on
which the Baptism of our Lord is celebrated, i.e. the*

Sunday occurring after 6 January, the readings of the weeks of the year are begun, omitting any which remain of those assigned to the ferias between 7-12 January.

	Year 1	Year 2
Jan 7 *or Mon. after Epiphany*	Is 61:1-11	Is 54:1-17
Jan. 8 *or Tues. after Epiphany*	Is 62:1-12	Is 55:1-13
Jan. 9 *or Wed. after Epiphany*	Is 63:7-64:1	Is 56:1-8
Jan. 10 *or Thurs. after Epiphany*	Is 64:1-12	Is 59:15-21
Jan. 11 *or Fri. after Epiphany*	Is 65:13-25	Bar 4:5-29
Jan. 12 *or Sat. after Epiphany*	Is 66:5-14a, 18-23	Bar 4:30-5:9

Sunday occurring after Jan. 6: Feast of the Baptism of our Lord   Is 42:1-8; 49:1-9

Lent

	Year 1	Year 2
Ash Wednesday	Is 58:1-14	
Thursday	Dt 1:1, 6-18	Ex 1:1-22
Friday	Dt 4:1-8, 32-40	Ex 2:1-22
Saturday	Dt 5:1-22	Ex 3:1-20

Week I

	Year 1	Year 2
Sunday	Dt 6:4-25	Ex 5:1-6:1
Monday	Dt 7:6-14; 8:1-6	Ex 6:2-13
Tuesday	Dt 9:7-21, 25-29	Ex 6:29-7:24
Wednesday	Dt 10:12-11:7, 26-28	Ex 10:21-11:10
Thursday	Dt 12:1-14	Ex 12:1-20
Friday	Dt 15:1-18	Ex 12:21-36

Saturday	Dt 16:1-17	Ex 12:37-49; 13:11-16

Week II

Sunday	Dt 18:1-22	Ex 13:17-14:9
Monday	Dt 24:1-25:4	Ex 14:10-31
Tuesday	Dt 26:1-19	Ex 16:1-18, 35
Wednesday	Dt 29:2-6, 10-29	Ex 17:1-16
Thursday	Dt 30:1-20	Ex 18:13-27
Friday	Dt 31:1-15, 23	Ex 19:1-19; 20:18-21
Saturday	Dt 32:48-52; 34:1-12	Ex 20:1-17

Week III

Sunday	Heb 1:1-2:4	Ex 22:20-23:9
Monday	Heb 2:5-18	Ex 24:1-18
Tuesday	Heb 3:1-19	Ex 32:1-5, 15-34
Wednesday	Heb 4:1-13	Ex 33:7-11, 18-23; 34:5-9, 29-35
Thursday	Heb 4:14-5:10	Ex 34:10-28
Friday	Heb 5:11-6:8	Ex 35:30-36:1; 37:1-9
Saturday	Heb 6:9-20	Ex 40:16-38

Week IV

Sunday	Heb 7:1-11	Lv 8:1-17; 9:22-24
Monday	Heb 7:11-28	Lv 16:2-27
Tuesday	Heb 8:1-13	Lv 19:1-18, 31-37
Wednesday	Heb 9:1-14	Lv 26:3-17, 38-46
Thursday	Heb 9:15-28	Nm 3:1-13; 8:5-11
Friday	Heb 10:1-10	Nm 9:15-10:10, 33-36
Saturday	Heb 10:11-25	Nm 11:4-6, 10-33

Week V

Sunday	Heb 10:26-39	Nm 12:1-15
Monday	Heb 11:1-19	Nm 12:16-13:3, 17-33
Tuesday	Heb 11:20-31	Nm 14:1-25
Wednesday	Heb 11:32-40	Nm 16:1-35
Thursday	Heb 12:1-13	Nm 20:1-13; 21:4-9
Friday	Heb 12:14-29	Nm 22:1-8a, 20-35
Saturday	Heb 13:1-25	Nm 24:1-19

Holy Week

Sunday	Is 50:4-51:3	Jer 22:1-8; 23:1-8
Monday	Is 52:13-53:12	Jer 26:1-15
Tuesday	Lam 1:1-12, 18-20	Jer 8:13-9:9
Wednesday	Lam 2:1-10	Jer 11:18-12:13
Thursday	Lam 2:11-22	Jer 15:10-21
Friday	Lam 3:1-33	Jer 16:1-15
Saturday	Lam 5:1-22	Jer 20:7-18

Eastertide

Easter Sunday *(Any one of the Vigil readings may be used)*

	Year 1	Year 2
Easter Week		
Monday	1 Pt 1:1-21	Acts 1:1-26
Tuesday	1 Pt 1:22-2:10	Acts 2:1-21
Wednesday	1 Pt 2:11-25	Acts 2:22-41
Thursday	1 Pt 3:1-17	Acts 2:42-3:11
Friday	1 Pt 3:18-4:11	Acts 3:12-4:4
Saturday	1 Pt 4:12-5:14	Acts 4:5-31
Week II		
Sunday	Col 3:1-17	Col 3:1-17
Monday	Rv 1:1-20	Acts 4:32-5:16
Tuesday	Rv 2:1-11	Acts 5:17-42
Wednesday	Rv 2:12-29	Acts 6:1-15

Thursday	Rv 3:1-22	Acts 7:1-16
Friday	Rv 4:1-11	Acts 7:17-43
Saturday	Rv 5:1-14	Acts 7:44-8:3

Week III

Sunday	Rv 6:1-17	Acts 8:4-25
Monday	Rv 7:1-17	Acts 8:26-40
Tuesday	Rv 8:1-13	Acts 9:1-22
Wednesday	Rv 9:1-12	Acts 9:23-43
Thursday	Rv 9:13-21	Acts 10:1-33
Friday	Rv 10:1-11	Acts 10:34-11:4, 18
Saturday	Rv 11:1-19	Acts 11:19-30

Week IV

Sunday	Rv 12:1-17	Acts 12:1-23
Monday	Rv 13:1-18	Acts 12:24-13:14a
Tuesday	Rv 14:1-13	Acts 13:14b-43
Wednesday	Rv 14:14-15:4	Acts 13:44-14:7
Thursday	Rv 15:5-16:21	Acts 14:8-15:4
Friday	Rv 17:1-18	Acts 15:5-35
Saturday	Rv 18:1-20	Acts 15:36-16:15

Week V

Sunday	Rv 18:21-19:10	Acts 16:16-40
Monday	Rv 19:11-21	Acts 17:1-18
Tuesday	Rv 20:1-15	Acts 17:19-34
Wednesday	Rv 21:1-8	Acts 18:1-28
Thursday	Rv 21:9-27	Acts 19:1-20
Friday	Rv 22:1-9	Acts 19:21-41
Saturday	Rv 22:10-21	Acts 20:1-16

Week VI

Sunday	1 Jn 1:1-10	Acts 20:17-38
Monday	1 Jn 2:1-11	Acts 21:1-26
Tuesday	1 Jn 2:12-17	Acts 21:27-39
Wednesday	1 Jn 2:18-29	Acts 21:40-22:21
Thursday	The ascension of Our Lord	Eph 4:1-24

| Friday | 1 Jn 3:1-10 | Acts 22:22-23:11 |
| Saturday | 1 Jn 3:11-17 | Acts 23:12-35 |

Week VII

Sunday	1 Jn 3:18-24	Acts 24:1-27
Monday	1 Jn 4:1-10	Acts 25:1-27
Tuesday	1 Jn 4:11-21	Acts 26:1-32
Wednesday	1 Jn 5:1-12	Acts 27:1-20
Thursday	1 Jn 5:13-21	Acts 27:21-44
Friday	2 Jn	Acts 28:1-14
Saturday	3 Jn	Acts 28:15-31

Pentecost Sunday   Rm 8:5-27

COMMON PRAYERS

THE APOSTLES' CREED

I believe in God, the Father almighty,
  creator of heaven and earth.

I believe in Jesus Christ, his only Son, our Lord.
  He was conceived by the power of the Holy Spirit
    and born of the Virgin Mary.
  He suffered under Pontius Pilate,
    was crucified, died, and was buried.
  He descended to the dead.
  On the third day he rose again.
  He ascended into heaven,
    and is seated at the right hand of the Father.
  He will come again to judge the living and the dead.

I believe in the Holy Spirit,
  the holy catholic Church,
  the communion of saints,
  the forgiveness of sins,
  the resurrection of the body,
  and the life everlasting.

THE LORD'S PRAYER

Our Father in heaven,
  holy be your Name,
  your kingdom come,
  your will be done,
    on earth as in heaven.
Give us today our daily bread.
Forgive us our sins
  as we forgive those who sin against us.
Do not bring us to the test
  but deliver us from evil.

For the kingdom, the power, and the glory are yours,
  now and for ever.

THE DOXOLOGY

Glory to the Father and to the Son and
    to the Holy Spirit:
  as in the beginning, so now, and for ever. Amen.

THE HAIL MARY

Hail, Mary, full of grace, the Lord is with you.
Blessed are you among women,
And blessed is the fruit of your womb, Jesus.
Holy Mary, Mother of God, pray for us sinners,
    now and at the hour of our death. Amen.

ACT OF CONTRITION

I confess to almighty God,
and to you, my brothers and sisters,
that I have sinned through my own fault
in my thoughts and in my words,
in what I have done,
and in what I have failed to do;
and I ask blessed Mary, ever-virgin,
all the angels and saints,
and you, my brothers and sisters,
to pray for me to the Lord our God.
—May almighty God have mercy on us,
  forgive us our sins,
    and bring us to everlasting life. Amen.

LIST OF PRAYERS, PSALMS AND CANTICLES

LIST OF PRAYERS, PSALMS AND CANTICLES

Canticle of Zachary   Lk 1:67-79

Antiphon . . .

Blessed be the Lord, the God of Israel;
   he has come to his people and set them free.
He has raised up for us a mighty Savior,
   born of the house of his servant David.

Through his holy prophets he promised of old
   that he would save us from our enemies,
   from the hands of all who hate us.
He promised to show mercy to our fathers
   and to remember his holy covenant.

This was the oath he swore to our father Abraham,
   to set us free from our enemies' hand,
free to worship him without fear,
   holy and righteous in his sight
   all the days of our life.

You, my child, shall be called the prophet of the Most
     High,
   for you will go before the Lord to prepare his way,
to give his people knowledge of salvation
   by forgiveness of their sins.

In the tender compassion of our God
   the dawn from on high shall break upon us,
to shine on those who dwell in darkness and the
     shadow of death,
   and to guide our feet on the road to peace.

Glory to the Father and to the Son and to the Holy
     Spirit;
   as in the beginning, so now, and for ever. Amen.

Antiphon . . .

Canticle of Mary   Lk 1:46-55

Antiphon . . .

My soul proclaims the greatness of the Lord,
    my spirit rejoices in God my Savior;
for he has looked with favor on his lowly servant,
    and from this day all generations will call me
        blessed.

The Almighty has done great things for me:
    holy is his name.
He has mercy on those who fear him
    in every generation.

He has shown the strength of his arm,
    he has scattered the proud in their conceit.
He has cast down the mighty from their thrones,
    and has lifted up the lowly.
He has filled the hungry with good things,
    and sent the rich away empty-handed.

He has come to the help of his servant Israel,
    for he remembered his promise of mercy,
the promise he made to our fathers,
    to Abraham and his children for ever.

Glory to the Father and to the Son and to the Holy
        Spirit;
    as in the beginning, so now, and forever. Amen.

Antiphon . . .